KAFFE FASSETT'S quilt road

Patchwork and Quilting book number 7

featuring Janet Bolton • Keiko Goke • Roberta Horton • Mary Mashuta • Liza Prior Lucy • Pauline Smith • Brandon Mably • Betsy Mennesson • Hilde Krohg

A ROWAN PUBLICATION

Currents, *Mossy Radiation* and *Romantic Rosy Quilts*
below West Yorkshire farmland.

First Published in Great Britain in 2005 by
Rowan Yarns
Green Lane Mill
Holmfirth
West Yorkshire
England
HD9 2DX

10 9 8

Art Director: Kaffe Fassett
Technical Editors: Ruth Eglinton and Pauline Smith
Co-ordinator: Pauline Smith
Editorial Director: Kate Buller
Patchwork Designs: Kaffe Fassett, Liza Prior Lucy, Pauline Smith,
                       Roberta Horton, Mary Mashuta,
                       Brandon Mably, Janet Bolton, Keiko Goke,
                       Hilde Aanerud Krohg and Betsy Mennesson.

Quilters: Judy Irish
Sewer: sewer for Roberta Horton and Mary Mashuta
                       quilts, Andrea Graham
Photography: Debbie Patterson
Flat shot photography: Dave Tolson @ Visage

Styling: Kaffe Fassett
Design Layout: Christine Wood - Gallery of Quilts/
                                         front section
                       Simon Wagstaff - instructions &
                                         technical information
Illustrations: Ruth Eglinton
Feature: Susan Berry

British Library Cataloguing in Publication Data
Rowan Yarns
Patchwork and Quilting
ISBN: 1-904485-40-5

Colour reproduction by Chroma Graphics (Overseas) Pte. Ltd
Printed and bound in Singapore by KHL. Printing Co. Pte. Ltd

contents

introduction

For this, the 7th book in my series for Rowan, the quilts have been photographed in Yorkshire. For years when I have visited the Rowan Mills I've been dazzled by the rich variation in the stone colours in the Yorkshire countryside. It was a great excitement for me to be able to use this backdrop for these very colourful quilts, because it provides the ideal neutral but very varied palette that sets them off so brilliantly, with a unique darkness that makes the colours in the quilt really glow.

We have this time added some great new fabrics to the range. It is the first time we have used other designers for the collection. They have produced a fresh bunch of new designs for us. Martha Negley's use of fruits & veggies caught my eye right away! They come in sumptuous colours, with a very voluptuous feel. Martha's *Dahlia* is one of my favourites - so overblown. There is simplicity in her approach to form which reminds me of old 1940's posters which are ideal for fabric design.

Elegant designs have come from Carla Miller, who does beautiful Old World colours on her marbled prints. They were worked out on computer and it is the first time that I have been won over by the use of a computer because they capture the subtle old end paper look. One of her patterns - *Fossil* - works well as a solid.

We have also brought in the Lille Collection, which come from a wonderful antique book of 19th century book of French prints that we purchased at a textile fair in New York. This time we have done five designs from the book and are planning to do many more.

The colour palette in the Lille collection is very strong. Most of the original paintings in the book are in soft blues and maroon, or in a neutral colour palette, so I went to the other extreme and recreated them in striking colours: for example, a very, very hot magenta on bright tobacco brown, and a deep violet on duck egg blue, not a bright duck egg blue but an electric duck egg blue, and a very hot lime jumping out from taupe. They are unusual colour combinations and wonderful to work with. I have just cut out my first quilt with these pieces.

One of my favourite designs is a tall leafy pattern called *Arbour*. It is a strikingly up-scale print that I have coloured in a strange high palette. I have just used this in a quilt for the first time and I can see that it cuts up beautifully. Large prints, in fact, run against the philosophy of many patchwork people who have tended not to use anything other than small or medium sized prints. The given wisdom is that people want a little scattering of motifs in all the pieces cut, but my feeling is a bit different. I like a quarter of a rose coming into a piece part of a leaf. The abstractness it creates is exciting and also using bigger squares that show a whole repeat of a blowsy floral or leaf print can be wonderfully dramatic. Having said that I also love small prints and repetition and combine these with my big prints.

Kaffe Fassett

the fabrics

One of the things that I think people are going to notice that I have done in this collection is to introduce a lot of yellow-based prints, a lot of red-based prints, and a lot of duck-egg blue slanted prints because I like to build a collection in a quilt of similar moods and then see the subtle differences within the print.

A girl who advised me when I first got interested in patchwork advised me to use contrast: "You want your darks, mediums and your lights to make it work", and by lights she meant white, and darks that were very dark. I have never really gone for that. Mostly I want beautiful merging colours so that each just slightly rises above the neighbouring patch and is very close toned. Lots of people have difficulty with tone and colour and confuse the two. The prints in our range have a lot of similar colour values that should make the quilt designer's job a delight.

There are themes and colour schemes that run through my own collection of new prints, which includes *Lotus Leaf* - a favourite, inspired by a Japanese ceramic garden seat. I bought an antique painted kimono with peonies on it that inspired a fabric called *Kimono* which has some very unexpected colours, like the rich cobalt blue peonies, which I used for the backing of the Mossy Radiation Quilt. In fact, I generally tend to go for big intense flowers, full of life, voluptuous. Floral Checkerboard Quilt showcases these fabrics a treat.

Two other new prints *Spools* and *Beachballs* are used to great effect in Liza's Romantic Rosy Quilt. The idea for *Spools*, as the name suggests, came from the round ends of spools of yarn on a shelf. I think this is going to be a really useful design with six colourways. *Beachballs* is a new play on stripes, twisting them into pinwheels. It's exciting to cut and sew.

Great new stripes we've added to the Indian hand wovens are *Single Ikat Feathers* in six unusual colourways. *Awning* is the other new stripe in some dusty colour combinations. I just had to do a bold stripy number; Chevrons Quilt is the result...quite easy and quick to make.

Another new fabric in my collection is *Confetti*, which is our first batik from India. It is purposely random so that each piece you cut is totally different from any other. It's made by a wax resist process, in which nails are hammered into a board, then dipped in wax and pressed into the fabric. The wax is then removed; traditionally this is done by soaking the fabric in boiling water. The random nature of the technique gives it a unique play on polka dot. The best use of *Confetti* in this book is in my Light and Dark Checkerboard Quilt and Brandon's My Fair Lady Quilt, which was inspired by the parasols in the film.

It's exciting to layer all the rich colours of our latest collection of quilts.

This time, as before, Liza Prior Lucy has been working with me on the collection.

According to Liza

" When I got the first "strike-offs" of Martha Negley's fruit and vegetable fabrics and the intensely colored Lille Collection, it occurred to me that the boldness of the fabric needed to be featured. I went back to the first quilt pattern that Kaffe and I made together, called Rosy. Because every other block in Rosy is plain and not pieced, large-scale prints can really show off. It was the perfect format to use the new bold veggies and flowers. I chose the darkest versions of these fabrics for Romantic Rosy Quilt because I had a need for a little dramatic color. The fabric arrived during the dankest, snowiest month and I was getting pretty tired of grey.

Kaffe and I have had an interesting year helping Rowan expand the fabric line by finding new designers. We have worked closely with this first group handpicking through wonderful artwork to find just the right designs that we would like to have put onto fabric.

The first version of Postcard is one that Kaffe worked on with me and he had chosen colors that were pulled from a favorite painting of his. For some reason, the colors sparkled in the painting but didn't in the quilt, so we worked and re-worked the palette until it looked beautiful. The whole time I was working on it, I was thinking how much I would like to see it in the colors of stones and marbles because the pattern reminded me of the floor in the center of Westminster Abbey.

When Carla Miller's strike-offs arrived, I found just the right selection of colors and prints to give this idea a try. By selecting the colors and patterns that most resembled natural stone colors - the pink, rust, red, turquoise, fuchsia and charcoal in *Lava*, *Dot Cube*, *Marble*, *Fossil*, and *Chicken Scratch* - I think I achieved my goal.

TOP LEFT A detail of the original Leafy Rosy Quilt from Kaffe Fassett Patchwork published by Ebury Press.
BOTTOM LEFT Romantic Rosy Quilt
OPPOSITE Liza's unfinished version of Postcard quilt in Carla Miller fabrics.

My friend Rebekah Lynch has taken the same quilt pattern for a third version.

I sent her samples of all the newest fabrics and she chose her absolute favorite combo, a riot of pinks and reds with just a touch of lime. From Kaffe's new fabrics she has chosen red *Leaves*, *Spools*, *Kimono* and *Lotus Leaf*, and new colourways of *Paperweight* in Gypsy and Paprika. She has dipped into the Lille Collection for *Nosegay*, *Flower Spray*, and *Dotted leaf*, whilst from Martha Negley she has made excellent use of red *Vegetable Leaves* to frame the nine-patch border.

As you can see this medallion style quilt is kind of a sampler and is a lot of fun to play with. Each border brings new surprises. We hope the different colorways we have come up with will inspire you to try one too. I am sure I will give it a whirl again, maybe in yellows. Yeah, yellows. What fun!"

Although unfinished, we just had to show the alternative colourways of Liza's Postcard Quilt.
N.B. Only the original Postcard Quilt in blues is a project in this book.

Liza's pink, ochre and green version in Carla Miller fabrics and Rebekah's red, pink and orange version both use the same pattern as the original blue one, so use the pattern and templates for the blue Postcard then follow the lead shown in the photos using your own mix of Carla Miller fabrics or a collection of fabrics in reds, pinks and oranges.

Further information will be available from Westminster Fibers for American quilters and Rowan for the rest of the world, or contact your nearest Rowan fabric stockist.

Rebekah's unfinished version of Liza's Postcard Quilt.

Crosses Quilt by Kaffe Fassett

The *Crosses Quilt* glowing on the moss covered Yorkshire stone. I love the way the crosses slightly merge and then appear sharply in places. The antique *Zinnia* border melts wonderfully into the old stone.

Romantic Rosy Quilt
by Liza Prior Lucy
Liza's *Romantic Rosy* is a rich,
new take on one of my first
quilt layouts. The deep palette
of the new fabrics is very
warming in the cool Yorkshire
spring.

Blue Arrows Quilt by Kaffe Fassett
I always have a soft spot for Islamic blue palettes. Here I've combined the blues in the graphic layout with deep toned

All Season Garden Quilt by Mary Mashuta
Mary Mashuta's *All Season Garden* is sumptuous indeed in this mossy garden setting.

My Fair Lady Quilt by Brandon Mably
Brandon's *My Fair Lady* uses slate Confetti fabric elegantly indeed - I love the way
the pastel motifs come and go in this grey softness.

Parterre Quilt by Pauline Smith
Pauline's *Parterre Quilt* is so romantic cascading down from this lush, pink shrub.
The moss on the stones relates well to my Wild Rose print.

Chevrons Quilt by Kaffe Fassett
It was so exciting to take our bold stripe range and do this simple graphic quilt. I love the way it
looks in this Yorkshire lane

Wallpaper Strips Quilt by Kaffe Fassett
How creamy the Wallpaper Strips Quilt turned out. We reversed some of the prints to give
an overall faded quality The magnolia tree gave us the perfect setting

Currents Quilt by Kaffe Fassett
This very graphic quilt is one of my favourites in this collection. My sister Kim and I hand quilted it in colourful running stitches. Pauline backed it in great bands of my Indian Stripes with thrilling effect.

Rowan's Baby Blocks Quilt by Keiko Goke

Patchwork Cats by Keiko Goke

Keiko Goke's dazzling quilt and cats use the brightest colours in our range. I love the way she backs that cat in Kimono print.

Light and Dark Checkerboard Quilt by Kaffe Fassett
This simple quilt is based on an antique I bought and love to sleep under. There is a gorgeous calmness about the regular checkerboard with its' slightly paler centre. I love the way it looks on the side of Rowan's mill.

En Kopp Te Til Kaffe Quilt by Hilde Aanerud Krohg
Hilde Aanerud Krohg from Norway attended my class in Holland and produced such an elegant piece we invited her to do this design. Its' quiet wit should inspire many a quilter. The embroidery matches her beautifully balanced choice of fabrics.

African Huts Quilt By Pauline Smith

Pauline's exciting palette for *African Huts Quilt* glows against these dark Yorkshire walls. Her use of

Kaleidoscope Cushion by Betsy Mennesson with *Postcard Quilt* by Liza Prior Lucy
Liza's *Postcard Quilt* gives people who like lots of piecing a good work out. It took the cool colours from an early still life I painted. The quilting on Betsy's cushion echoes the veins in my lotus leaf print.

Floral Checkerboard Quilt by Kaffe Fassett

I'm totally in awe of these huge moss covered trees. The *Floral Checkerboard* looks quite at home with its' warm green and pastel colouring

Mossy Radiation Quilt by Kaffe Fassett
I designed this quilt with as many mossy tones as I could find in my new collection so it would work in this northern English spring. Weren't we lucky to find this elegantly peeling green shed to show it on! The cobalt *Kimono* adds an electric note as the quilt backing.

Rose Cottage Quilt by Roberta Horton
Roberta's rather ghostly *Rose Cottage Quilt* looks great against the farm buildings. The crimson *Wild Rose* print looks amazing next to the dark hen house.

Two Birds in a Sunny Garden Panel by Janet Bolton
Janet Bolton's witty statement in the shot cotton range is perfectly at home on this old mill door.

When we invited Janet to accept a commission to design and sew a panel for the book we held our breath until she had handled and approved the fabrics we sent her. If she didn't like them or feel she could work with them she would decline our invitation. We were thrilled when she accepted. For this book she has worked for the first time with prescribed fabrics. In her light first floor studio she handles the fine cottons that Kaffe Fassett has coloured and patterned. From the wonderful selection of these delicious colours she has created an abstract fishpond with floating leaves and birds flying above titled 'Two Birds In A Sunny Garden' that takes her back to the broad spaces of the Lancashire/Yorkshire border where she grew up.

A Personal Approach

Janet Bolton's work constantly returns to the North of her childhood – a wonderful time in the village of Feniscowles, now a part of Blackburn, where, with her friends, she was free to run in the fields and explore the streams and countryside in a way that is rare today. They gathered leaves and collected seeds and spent hours arranging them in patterns and writing labels. The cows, the sheep, the mills, are all images that come from this time and are worked in a similar way to that early pattern making. (see *On Top of the World* and *Three Ladies with One Yellow Kiite*)

On Top of the World

The idyllic freedom of village life was punctuated by visits to the local market town where her father would take her and her mother to visit his tailor and then to the boutiques at Southport where new dresses were chosen for her mother. This always centred on the fabrics, swatches that her father would handle and feel - of grey stuff for his suits and lengths of fine silks for his wife's dresses - whilst her mother sat and nodded her approval at his choice. When the shopping was done they would have afternoon tea in grand style at the nearby hotel.

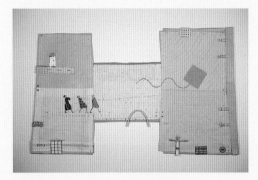

Three Ladies with One Yellow Kiite

Her father, a successful manufacturer of paint, brought his children up to be responsible citizens. He arranged their education – private until they had passed the 11+ when they could choose where to go next - and made sure they were able to look after themselves. For Janet, the youngest, this meant the gift of a hat shop to set her up in business and keep her happy until she married. But Janet although quiet and rather shy, was at heart rebellious. The grammar school in Darwen, where she chose to be educated, was co-educational with some politically left-wing teachers. Early glimmers of feminism helped her decline his gift and with great certainty decide instead on a two year Foundation Course at the Harris School of Art in Preston, which she loved. This led to a Fine Art Diploma after a course chosen because it included silk-screen printing on fabric - as well as lithography and etching – a process that she later realised she didn't like because it lacked the simple directness of handling the fabric.

After this she was guided by her father's practical wish that she should complete a teachers' training course in Liverpool 'just in case'. And it was while she was doing her probationary teaching year in London that she chanced to visit the Crane Kalman Gallery, around the corner from the Victoria & Albert Museum in Knightsbridge, and saw the collage pictures by Elizabeth Allen, a seamstress, that told stories using fabric. This gave her the idea of picture-making with fabric rather than paint. As well as teaching she began making pictures and patch-worked curtains and cushions for the flat that she and her new husband, Paul, shared in south London. Soon her two children, Fran and Al were born, so she stayed at home and had more time for the picture making.

In time she took stands in local craft markets in Dulwich and Greenwich where celebrities were amongst her buyers. She was excited by the sales – thrilled that someone wanted to buy what she had made initially just for herself. With this encouragement she stopped making cushion covers and useful objects and concentrated on creating the textile pictures for which she is now known internationally. In 1984 she was invited to show at the Chelsea Crafts Fair, where on the first day a group of American buyers came to her stand and bought every piece.

Two Hens in the Hayfield

The American market has always appreciated her work – the simplicity of the stitching and imagery that belies the time and thought that goes into every piece. Americans in particular love the naïve redrawing of birds and animals with fabrics, that is so like parts of their Folk Art (*see Two Hens in the Hayfield* and *Two Black Hens)* and they take it seriously, academically. In England we tend to disregard Folk Art in favour of art made on the easel and it is often hard for makers to earn a living. But Janet was brought up with an old fashioned business ethic; she was taught never to borrow and always to pay bills; to nurture a pride in what she did and 'keep her feet on the ground'. This has meant that she has taken opportunities as they come, but taken them with care. At Chelsea she was asked to do a series of cards for Gallery Five and this was followed by several offers of books. She has enjoyed learning how books are laid out and produced, at times making drawings and paintings to illustrate her methods, but she knows that her real love is to sit quietly and work on the pictures.

Two Black Hens

This quietness in cutting and placing and sewing the fabrics by hand, before catching the buttons, sticks or tiny objects with hand stitching, produces a calmness in the pictures that helps us to conjure our own memories of childhood. Often when she has worked on a piece for some time, she will live with it for a while before taking something away, and then it is finished and ready for its simple title.

As well as her successes in the US, her work can be seen in many different places throughout the British Isles - she exhibits in both fine art and craft galleries. She regularly shows work at Contemporary Applied Arts, the UK's leading craft gallery in central London where I was Director until recently. She has shown alongside antiques in shops, and with embroiderers and quilters at craft fairs. This ability for the work to cross boundaries has given many different people the opportunity to become familiar with it and to share Janet's sheer joy in playing with colour and fabric.

For Janet the fabrics must be woven as she is acutely aware of the feel and the structure of each material that she uses. She likes the fine cotton lawns that can be manipulated to form the sheep and chicken and other images. She describes this as 'drawing with the fabric' and notes its quality by its ability to be tucked and pulled

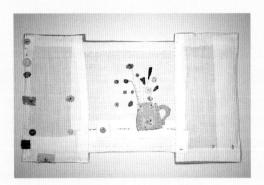

Flowers in May

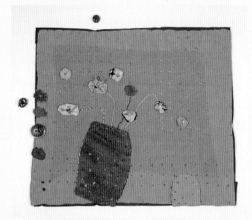

The Red Flower Vase

Ballooning Over the Hills, Castle

to the required shape. The heavier cottons and silks she uses only for the backgrounds. Sometimes she recycles a piece from a fine lawn handkerchief (see *Flowers in May*) so that one can see the colour coming through from underneath. She likes the fineness of the thinned fabric because it reminds her of times in her childhood when she would wear a much washed and loved hand-me-down dress. This delicacy of the lawn reflects the few wild flowers in the handled mug and Janet draws these to our attention by the neat folding under of the nearby fabric to frame the image.

In much of Janet's work one is aware of the English colours, the pale grey skies, the washed out hills and landscapes, the colder light of the north. Sometimes, though, she works in bolder colours and recently she has introduced strong greens that she had never ever used before. The picture of the vase of wild flowers (see *The Red Flower Vase*) is intensified by the green background and further highlighted by the three bright red buttons.

When she travels she collects fabrics and makes colour sketches of what she sees around her and these images become part of her memory. It takes maybe five years for these influences to perculate through into the work or for her to feel confident to find a way to use particular fabrics. The castle on the hill at Launceston in Cornwall, where she runs workshops each summer, appears in her picture of the ballooners. (see *Ballooning Over the Hills, Castle*) Janet is a generous maker. She runs workshops to share her skills and to encourage others to find time to quietly sew something by hand and thus bring back all sorts of memories. She likes to pass on her experiences believing that people have a natural instinct to make things. As she remarks with feeling 'The world would be a better place if more people had a go at making things.'

Blue Bird Visiting the Flowers

To see more of Janet's work visit
http://www.gaylewillson.com and click on the
Janet Bolton link.

Janet Bolton's Books

- *Black Cat in the Bedroom.* Bloomsbury, 1997
  ISBN: 0747528454

- *Green Frog in the Sitting Room*, 1997
  ISBN: 0747528462

- *Speckled Hen in the Kitchen*, 1997
  ISBN: 0747528470

- *White Goose in the Bathroom*, 1997
  ISBN:0747528446

- *In a Patchwork Garden*, Museum Quilts
  Publications, 1996
  ISBN: 1897954417

- *Mrs Noah's Patchwork Quilt*, Tango Books, 1995
  SBN: 1857070836

- *Patchwork Folk Art*, Museum Quilts Publications,
  1995
  ISBN: 0806913207

© Mary La Trobe-Bateman
Mary La Trobe Bateman OBE is a freelance consultant
and curator. She recently retired after ten years as
Director of Contemporary Applied Arts, the award
winning gallery in central London. She is a trustee of
The Making, a selector for COLLECT at the V&A and
sits on committees for the Goldsmiths' Company and
the Crafts Council.

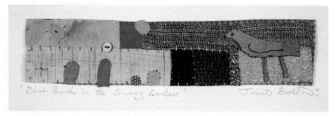

Blue Bird in the Sunny Garden

Two Hens at Harvest Time

Two Hares Listening

Pale Bird in the Blue Night

African Huts Quilt ★

PAULINE SMITH

These simple picture blocks could be embellished with appliqué, embroidery and fancy quilting to create your own African village.

SIZE OF QUILT
The finished quilt will measure approx.
40in x 40in (102cm x 102cm).

MATERIALS
Patchwork Fabrics:
BATIK CONFETTI

Tomato	BKC01:	½yd (45cm) includes binding

DOUBLE IKAT POLKA

Pumpkin	DIP02:	¼yd (25cm)
Blue	DIP05:	¼yd (25cm)

SINGLE IKAT FEATHERS

Curry	SIF01:	¼yd (25cm)
Earth	SIF02:	¼yd (25cm)
Storm	SIF03:	¼yd (25cm)
Raspberry	SIF06:	¼yd (25cm)

SINGLE IKAT WASH

Banana	SIW03:	⅜yd (30cm)
Red	SIW06:	¼yd (25cm)

SHOT COTTON

Ginger	SC01:	¼yd (25cm)
Prune	SC03:	⅛yd (15cm)
Raspberry	SC08:	⅛yd (15cm)
Chartreuse	SC12:	¼yd (25cm)
Denim	SC15:	⅛yd (15cm)
Smoke	SC20:	¼yd (25cm)
Mushroom	SC31:	¼yd (25cm)

Backing Fabric: 1¼yds (1.2m)
We suggest these fabrics for backing:
DOUBLE IKAT POLKA Blue DIP05
SINGLE IKAT FEATHERS Curry SIF01
SINGLE IKAT WASH Banana SIW03

Binding:
BATIK CONFETTI
Tomato BKC01: see patchwork fabrics

Batting:
44in x 44in (112cm x 112cm).

Quilting thread:
Toning machine quilting thread.

Templates:
see page 102, 103.

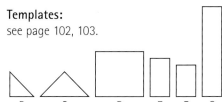

PATCH SHAPES
Each block in this quilt is based around a large square patch shape (Template D) used for the main hut wall. The roof of the hut is made in 2 ways, with either 4 small triangles (Template B) or 2 small triangles (Template B) and 1 large triangle (Template C). The background is made using 3 rectangle patch shapes (Templates E, F & G).

CUTTING OUT
Note: Cut the template patch shapes in the order specified. Reserve leftover fabric strips for following templates and trim as necessary.

Template B: Cut 3⅝in (9.25cm) wide strips across the width of the fabric. Each strip will give you 22 patches per 45in (114cm) wide fabric. Cut 8 in SIW03, SC08, 7 in SC03, SC20, 4 in DIP02, DIP05, 2 in BKC01, SIW06, SC01, SC12, SC15 & SC31.

Template C: Cut 3⅜in (8.5cm) wide strips across the width of the fabric. Each strip will give you 11 patches per 45in (114cm) wide fabric. Cut 4 in SC20, 2 in SC01 & 1 in SC12.

Template D: Cut 5½in (14cm) wide strips across the width of the fabric. Each strip will give you 7 patches per 45in (114cm) wide fabric. Cut 5 in SIF02, SIF03, 4 in SIF06 & 2 in SIF01.

Template E: Cut 2¾in (7cm) wide strips across the width of the fabric. Each strip will give you 10 patches per 45in (114cm) wide fabric. Cut 8 in SIW03, 4 in DIP02, DIP05, SC03, 2 in BKC01, SIW06, SC08, SC15, SC20 & SC31.

Template F: Cut 2¾in (7cm) wide strips across the width of the fabric. Each strip will give you 9 patches per 45in (114cm) wide fabric. Cut 6 in SIW06, 4 in BKC01, DIP02, DIP05, SIW03, SC12, SC31 & 2 in SC01.

Template G: Cut 2¾in (7cm) wide strips across the width of the fabric. Each strip will give you 4 patches per 45in (114cm) wide fabric. Cut 3 in SIW06, 2 in BKC01, DIP02, DIP05, SIW03, SC12, SC31 & 1 in SC01.

Binding: Cut 4 strips 2¹/₂in (6.5cm) wide x width of fabric in BKC01.

Backing: Cut 1 piece 44in x 44in (112cm x 112cm) in backing fabric.

MAKING THE QUILT
Use a ¹/₄in (6mm) seam allowance throughout. Refer to the quilt assembly diagram for fabric combinations. There are 2 ways to construct the hut roof sections, follow either diagram a or b, then complete the blocks using diagram c

and d. Piece a total of 16 blocks. Piece the blocks into 4 rows of 4 blocks then join the rows to form the quilt centre.

FINISHING THE QUILT
Press the quilt top. Layer the quilt top, batting and backing and baste together (see page 120). Using a toning machine quilting thread quilt-in-the-ditch around all the blocks, then as shown in the quilting diagram. Trim the quilt edges and attach the binding (see page 121).

Quilting Diagram

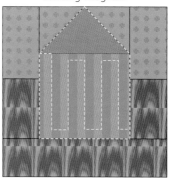

Block Assemby

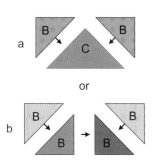

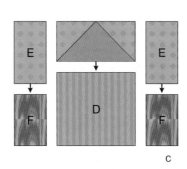

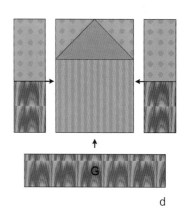

Quilt Assemby

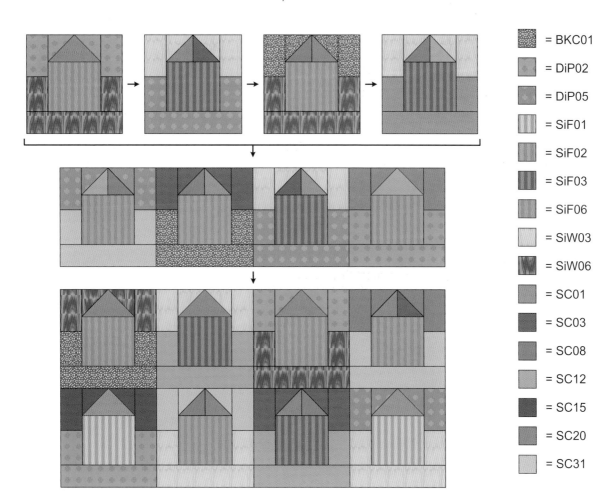

= BKC01
= DiP02
= DiP05
= SiF01
= SiF02
= SiF03
= SiF06
= SiW03
= SiW06
= SC01
= SC03
= SC08
= SC12
= SC15
= SC20
= SC31

All Season Garden Quilt ★★

Mary Mashuta

Ikat woven stripes are Mary's favourite because they look so sophisticated when they are cut and stitched in repetitive patterns. An antique strippy quilt gets a contemporary make-over with Kaffe's fabrics. As a stripe expert, Mary includes tips for accurate cutting and stitching.

SIZE OF QUILT
The finished quilt will measure approx. 58in x 64in (147.5cm x 162.5cm).

MATERIALS
Patchwork Fabrics:
LOTUS LEAF
Antique	GP29AN:	1/2yd (45cm)
Blue	GP29BL:	1/2yd (45cm)
Red	GP29RD:	1/2yd (45cm)

LEAVES
Black	GP30BK:	1/4yd (25cm)
Jade	GP30JA:	1/4yd (25cm)
Ochre	GP30OC:	1/4yd (25cm)
Red	GP30RD:	1/4yd (25cm)

SINGLE IKAT FEATHERS
Curry	SIF01:	1/2yd (45cm)
Storm	SIF03:	1/2yd (45cm)
Purple	SIF05:	1/2yd (45cm)
Raspberry	SIF06:	1/2yd (45cm)

Border Fabrics:
DOUBLE IKAT POLKA
Scarlet	DIP03:	1/4yd (25cm)

ZINNIA
Antique	GP31AN:	1/2yd (45cm)
Crimson	GP31CR:	1/2yd (45cm)

Backing Fabric: 3 7/8yds (3.6m)
We suggest these fabrics for backing:
ZINNIA Magenta GP31MG
LEAVES Red GP30RD
LOTUS LEAF Antique GP29AN
Leftover backing fabric can be used in the quilt.

Binding:
SHOT COTTON
Raspberry	SC08:	1/2yd (45cm)

Batting:
66in x 72in (168cm x 183cm).

Quilting thread:
Toning machine quilting thread
Contrasting machine quilting thread
Optional, perle cotton for borders.

Templates:
see page 108.

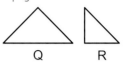

PATCH SHAPES
The quilt centre is made from four zig-zag strips pieced from 2 triangle patch shapes (Templates Q and R). They are alternated with long strips of floral fabric cut from 3 colourways of the same print. The quilt is finished with a border with corner posts.

CUTTING OUT
Important Information:
Please read carefully before cutting the stripe fabric triangles.
1. The grain placement and stripe pattern placement are important graphically and technically. (Accurate grain placement keeps fabric from stretching along the longest edge when sewing in strips and joining to floral strips later.)
2. Some pieces will need to be 'fussy' cut to read correctly visually.
3. You can only cut 1 layer of the stripe fabric at a time if stripes are to remain exactly on grain and be visually correct.
4. You may decide to cut a few extra stripe triangles so you can have more options in arranging them, a little extra yardage has been allowed for this.

Template R: LEAVES FABRICS: Cut 3 7/8in (10cm) wide strip across the width of the fabric. Cut 2 in GP30BK, GP30JA, GP30OC and GP30RD. Reserve leftover strip and trim for template Q.
Template Q: LEAVES FABRICS: Cut 3 5/8in (9.25cm) wide strips across the width of the fabric. Each strip will give you 10 patches per 45in (114cm) wide fabric. Cut 17 in GP30BK, GP30JA, GP30OC and GP30RD.
Template Q: STRIPE FABRICS: Carefully true-up the stripe fabrics so that the stripes are exactly perpendicular to the cut edge. From each of the striped fabrics cut 1 x 3 5/8in (9.25cm) wide strip across the width of the fabric. From this 'fussy' cut 9 triangles ensuring that each has a

dark stripe in the centre of the triangle as shown in Cutting Diagram A. Total 9 triangles in SIF01, SIF03, SIF05 and SIF06. From the remaining STRIPE FABRICS: Fussy cut 8 Template Q triangles along the length of the stripes, as shown in Cutting Diagram B. Each triangle should have a dark stripe along the sewing line of the long side. Total 8 in SIF01, SIF03, SIF05 and SIF06.
Template R: STRIPE FABRICS: Cut 2 in SIF01, SIF03, SIF05 and SIF06.

Floral Strips: From each of the floral fabrics cut 2 strips 8¹/₂in (21.5cm) x the width of the fabric, join as necessary. Cut 1 strip 8¹/₂in x 54¹/₂in (21.5cm x 138.5cm) from GP29AN, GP29BL and GP29RD.

Border: Cut 3 strips 5¹/₂in (14cm) x the width of the fabric, join as necessary. Cut 2 strips 5¹/₂in x 54¹/₂in (14cm x 138.5cm) in GP31AN Cut 3 strips 5¹/₂in (14cm) x the width of the fabric, join as necessary. Cut 2 strips

5¹/₂in x 48¹/₂in (14cm x 123.25cm) in GP31CR.

Corner Posts: Cut 4 squares 5¹/₂in x 5¹/₂in (14cm x 14cm) in DIP03.

Binding: Cut 6 strips 2¹/₂in (6.5cm) wide x width of fabric in SC08.

Backing: Cut 1 piece 44in x 66in (112cm x 168cm) and 1 piece 29in x 66in (74cm x 168cm) in backing fabric.

Cutting Diagram A

Cutting Diagram B

Quilt Assemby

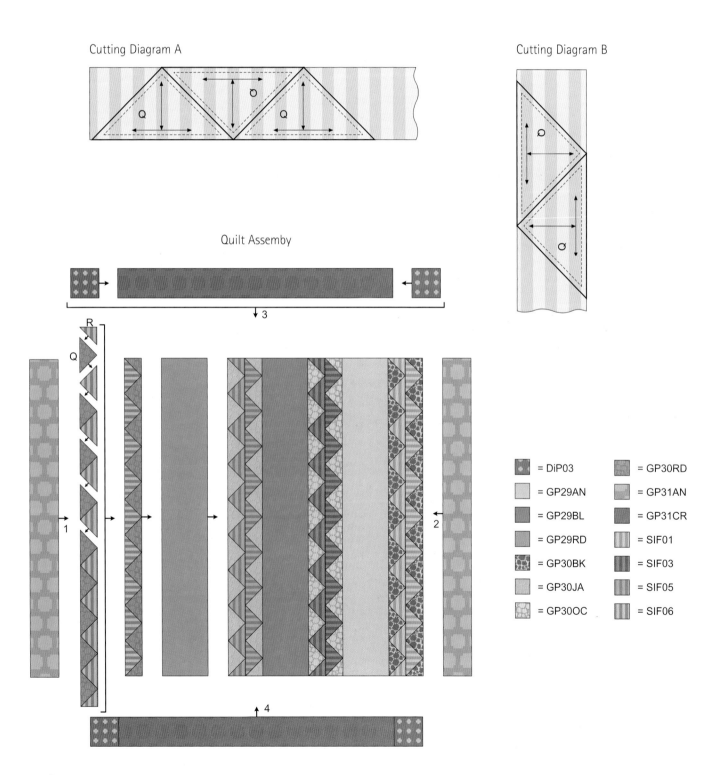

= DiP03	= GP30RD
= GP29AN	= GP31AN
= GP29BL	= GP31CR
= GP29RD	= SIF01
= GP30BK	= SIF03
= GP30JA	= SIF05
= GP30OC	= SIF06

MAKING THE ZIG-ZAG STRIPS

Use a ¼in (6mm) seam allowance throughout. Arrange all the stripe and leaves triangles in rows as shown in the diagram. You may want to fine tune the placement of the triangles before sewing. Join the triangles 2 at a time being careful not to stretch the bias edges. You may find it helpful to place 3 pins across each seam, gently place your finger on the pin to help guide it through your machine. Join the triangles to form rows and press the seams open. Join two strips of joined triangles being careful to create zig-zag patterns. (Mark the middle of each triangle with a pin to use as a guide in lining up the rows.) Press the seam towards the triangles with the stripe along the long side.

MAKING THE QUILT

Arrange the floral and pieced strips alternately as shown in the quilt assembly diagram, join to form the quilt centre. Add the side borders, join a corner post to each end of the top and bottom borders, add to the quilt centre.

FINISHING THE QUILT

Press the quilt top. Seam the backing pieces using a ¼in (6mm) seam allowance to form a piece approx. 66in x 72in (168cm x 183cm). Layer the quilt top, batting and backing and baste together (see page 120). Machine quilt in the ditch all the vertical and horizontal seams using toning thread. Following the quilting diagram quilt the zig-zag strips and floral strips as shown using contrasting thread. Mary suggests a longer quilting stitch to show off the contrasting thread. Machine quilt the borders in a zig-zag pattern or hand stitch the flowers with perle cotton if you prefer. Trim the quilt edges and attach the binding (see page 121).

Quilting Diagram

Blue Arrows Quilt ★ ★
KAFFE FASSETT

I used a simple layout of triangles as a vehicle for my palette of recent blue prints.

SIZE OF QUILT
The finished quilt will measure approx. 65½in x 85in (166cm x 216cm).

MATERIALS
Patchwork Fabrics:
DOUBLE IKAT POLKA

Denim	DIP04: ½yd (45cm)	
Blue	DIP05: ⅜yd (35cm)	

PAPERWEIGHT

Cobalt	GP20CB: 1 yd (90cm) includes binding	

SWIGGLE STRIPE

Blue	GP22BL: 2 yds (1.8m)	

PANSY

Blue	GP23BL: ½yd (45cm)

LEAVES

Blue	GP30BL: ½yd (45cm)

ZINNIA

Blue	GP31BL: ¾yd (70cm)
Crimson	GP31CR: ⅝yd (60cm)

KIMONO

Cobalt Turquoise	GP33CT: ½yd (45cm)

SHOT COTTON

Cobalt	SC45: 1 yd (90cm)
Aegean	SC46: ⅞yd (80cm)
Grape	SC47: ¾yd (70cm)

Backing Fabric: 5¼yds (4.8m)
We suggest these fabrics for backing: ZINNIA Crimson GP31CR or Blue GP31BL Leftover backing fabric can be used in the quilt.

Binding:
PAPERWEIGHT
Cobalt   GP20CB:
                see patchwork fabrics

Batting:
73in x 92in (186cm x 234cm).

Quilting thread:
Blue hand quilting thread.

Templates:
see page 103.

M   N

PATCH SHAPES
This quilt is made using 2 triangle patch shapes (Templates M & N). The larger triangle is pieced into rows with the smaller triangle used to fill in the ends of the rows. The rows are then joined to form the quilt.

CUTTING OUT
The Blue Swiggle Stripe fabric (GP22BL) has four distinct design elements. These have been separated and individually coloured in the quilt assembly diagram. Design Element 1 (striped buds), Design Element 2 (red blob on blue), Design Element 3 (blue stripes) and Design Element 4 (lilac swiggle on turquoise) are all used in this quilt.

Template M: Fabric GP22BL ONLY. Cut 3⅛in (8cm) wide strips down the length of the fabric, separating the design elements as you cut. Cut 40 in GP22BL Design Element 1,
39 in GP22BL Design Element 4,
31 in GP22BL Design Element 2 and
29 in GP22BL Design Element 3.
Template M: All other fabrics. Cut 3⅛in (8cm) wide strips across the width of the fabric. Each strip will give you 12 patches per 45in (114cm) wide fabric. Cut 98 in SC46, 88 in SC47, 84 in SC45, 76 in GP31BL, 65 in GP31CR, 52 in GP33CT, 49 in GP30BL, 47 in GP23BL, 43 in DIP04, 40 in GP20CB, 35 in DIP05.
Template N: Cut 3⅜in (8.5cm) wide strips across the width of the fabric. Each strip will give you 24 patches per 45in (114cm) wide fabric. Cut 68 in SC45.

Binding: Cut 8 strips 2½in (6.5cm) wide x width of fabric in GP20CB.

Backing: Cut 1 piece 44in x 92in (112cm x 234cm) and 1 piece 30in x 92in (76cm x 234cm) in backing fabric.

MAKING THE QUILT
Use a ¼in (6mm) seam allowance throughout and refer to the quilt assembly diagram for fabric arrangement. Piece a total of 34 rows, each row has 24 template M triangles and 2 Template N triangles for the row ends. Join the rows to form the quilt.

FINISHING THE QUILT
Press the quilt top. Seam the backing pieces using a ¼in (6mm) seam allowance to form a piece approx. 73in x 92in (186cm x 234cm). Layer the quilt top, batting and backing and baste together (see page 120). Hand quilt in diagonal rows as shown on the bottom right of the quilt assembly diagram using blue hand quilting thread. Trim the quilt edges and attach the binding (see page 121).

Quilt Assemby

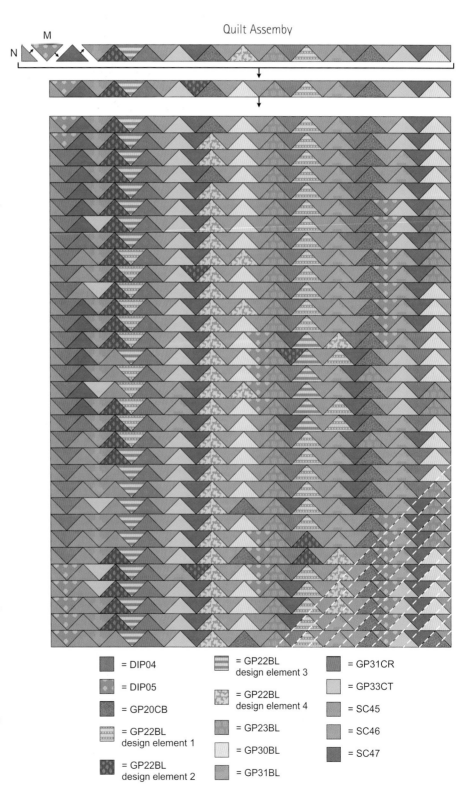

■ = DIP04

▦ = DIP05

■ = GP20CB

▦ = GP22BL design element 1

▨ = GP22BL design element 2

▦ = GP22BL design element 3

▧ = GP22BL design element 4

■ = GP23BL

▨ = GP30BL

■ = GP31BL

■ = GP31CR

□ = GP33CT

■ = SC45

■ = SC46

■ = SC47

Chevrons Quilt ★

KAFFE FASSETT

This bold, simple idea makes good use of our new Awning Stripe fabric, woven in India. It looks a lot more complex than the one basic triangle it employs.

SIZE OF QUILT
The finished quilt will measure approx.
84in x 84in (213cm x 213cm).

MATERIALS
Note: The fabrics chosen for this quilt are all fully reversible. The method given would not work for non-reversible fabrics
Patchwork Fabrics:
ALTERNATE STRIPE

AS10: 1/2yd (45cm)

AWNING STRIPE
Sage   AWS01: 1 yd (90cm)
Duck Egg   AWS03: 1 3/4yds (1.6m)
Lilac   AWS04: 1 yd (90cm)
Brown   AWS05: 3/4yd (70cm)
Midnight   AWS06: 3/4yd (70cm)
EXOTIC STRIPE

ES15: 3/4yd (70cm)

ES16: 1/2yd (45cm)
ES20: 3/4yd (70cm)
SINGLE IKAT FEATHERS
Earth   SIF02: 1/2yd (45cm)
Raspberry   SIF06: 3/4yd (70cm)

Backing Fabric: 5 1/4yds (4.8m)
Any of the patchwork fabrics listed above would be suitable to back this quilt.

Binding:
AWNING STRIPE
Sage   AWS01: 3/4yd (70cm)

Batting:
90in x 90in (229cm x 229cm).

Quilting thread:
Black machine quilting thread.

Templates:
see page 106.

PATCH SHAPES
A triangle patch shape (Template K) is pieced into square blocks to make up the centre of this quilt. The blocks are pieced into diagonal rows with the same triangle patch shape used to fill the ends of the rows. The extreme corners of the quilt are completed using a second triangle patch shape (Template L).

CUTTING OUT
Template L: Cut a 7 7/8in (20cm) strip from the width of the fabric in AWS03. From this cut 1 x 7 7/8in (20cm) square. Using the template as a guide cut the square twice diagonally to make 4 triangles. The remaining strip can be trimmed and used for template K.
Template K: Cut 7 1/2in (19cm) wide strips across the width of the fabric. Cut 7 1/2in (19cm) squares and then, using the template as a guide, cut each square diagonally to make 2 triangles, keep each pair of triangles together. Each strip will give you 10 patches per 45in (114cm) wide fabric. Cut 70 in AWS03, 32 in AWS01, AWS04, 30 in AWS05, ES15, 26 in SIF06, 24 in ES20, 22 in AWS06, 20 in SIF02, AS10 and 16 in ES16.

Binding: Cut 9 3/4yds (8.9m) of 2 1/2in (6.5cm) wide bias binding in AWS01.

Backing: Cut 2 pieces 45in x 90in (115cm x 229cm) in backing fabric.

MAKING THE BLOCKS
Use a 1/4in (6mm) seam allowance throughout. Reserve 32 template K triangles in AWS03 for the quilt edges, piece all the other template K triangles into blocks as follows. Referring to the block assembly diagram, take a pair of Template K triangles and lay on a flat surface as shown in diagram a. Take 1 of the triangles and flip it over as shown in diagram b, then match and stitch the two triangles together as shown in diagram c making sure the stripe directions now run at right angles. Make a total of 145 blocks.

MAKING THE QUILT

Join the blocks into diagonal rows as shown in the quilt assembly diagram, filling in the row ends with the reserved Template K triangles, and the extreme corners with Template L triangles. Handle the quilt very carefully as the edges are bias cut and a bit stretchy.

FINISHING THE QUILT

Press the quilt top. Seam the backing pieces using a 1/4in (6mm) seam allowance to form a piece approx. 90in x 90in (229cm x 229cm). Layer the quilt top, batting and backing and baste together (see page 120). Using black machine quilting thread quilt in a geometric pattern as shown in the quilting diagram loosely following the fabric stripes. Trim the quilt edges and attach the binding (see page 121).

Block Assembly Diagrams

a

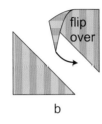
b

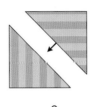
c

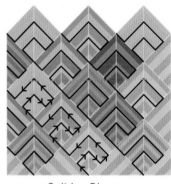

Quilting Diagram

Quilt Assembly

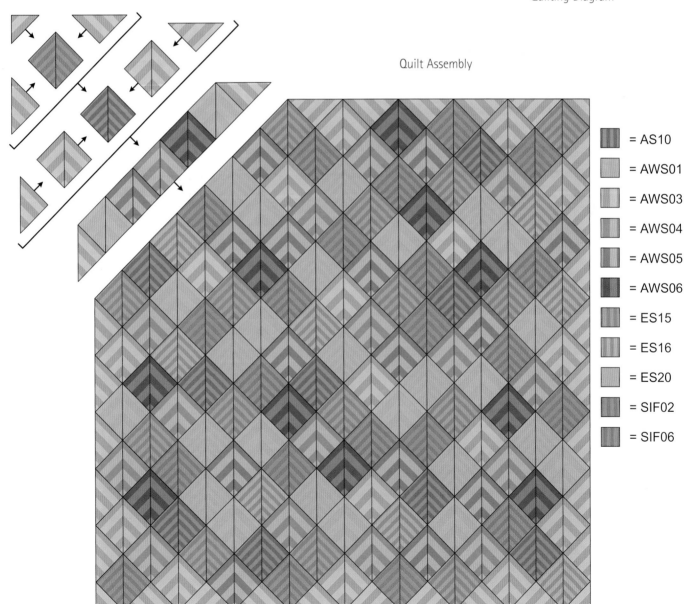

= AS10

= AWS01

= AWS03

= AWS04

= AWS05

= AWS06

= ES15

= ES16

= ES20

= SIF02

= SIF06

Crosses Quilt ★

Kaffe Fassett

This beautiful cross form that occurs in my favourite Russian ikons is an existing form for a quilt. The rich palette of multi-tones gives a carpet-like texture.

SIZE OF QUILT
The finished quilt will measure approx. 67in x 61in (170cm x 155cm).

MATERIALS
Patchwork Fabrics:
ROMAN GLASS
Gold	GP01G:	¹/₄yd (25cm)
Jewel	GP01J:	¹/₄yd (25cm)
Leafy	GP01L:	¹/₄yd (25cm)
Red	GP01R:	¹/₄yd (25cm)

FORGET ME NOT ROSE
Magenta	GP08MG:	¹/₄yd (25cm)

PAPERWEIGHT
Pumpkin	GP20PN:	¹/₄yd (25cm)

SWIGGLE STRIPE
Green	GP22GN:	³/₄yd (70cm)

PANSY
Blue	GP23BL:	¹/₄yd (25cm)

Brown	GP23BR:	¹/₄yd (25cm)
Gold	GP23GD:	¹/₄yd (25cm)

DIAGONAL POPPY
Duck Egg	GP24DE:	¹/₄yd (25cm)
Lavender	GP24LV:	¹/₄yd (25cm)

KASHMIR
Black	GP25BK:	¹/₄yd (25cm)

WILD ROSE
Crimson	GP26CR:	¹/₄yd (25cm)

ZINNIA
Blue	GP31BL:	¹/₄yd (25cm)

BATIK CONFETTI
Blue	BKC02:	¹/₄yd (25cm)
Moss	BKC03:	¹/₄yd (25cm)
Lilac	BKC06:	¹/₄yd (25cm)

DOUBLE IKAT POLKA
Scarlet	DIP03:	¹/₄yd (25cm)

PAISLEY STRIPE
Antique	GP32AN:	¹/₄yd (25cm)

Borders:
ZINNIA
Antique	GP31AN:	1⁷/₈yds (1.7m)

Backing Fabric: 3⁷/₈yds (3.6m)
We suggest these fabrics for backing:
NARROW STRIPE NS09 or NS17
Exotic Stripe	ES21

Binding:
AWNING STRIPE
Sage	AWS01:	⁵/₈yd (60cm)

Batting:
74in x 68in (188cm x 173cm).

Quilting thread:
Dark red machine quilting thread.

Templates:
see page 102.

J

PATCH SHAPES
A single square patch shape (Template J) is used for this quilt. It is the position of the fabrics which produces the interlocking crosses design. The quilt is framed with a simple border.

CUTTING OUT
The Green Swiggle Stripe fabric (GP22GN) has four distinct design elements, three are used in this quilt. They have been numbered in the quilt assembly diagram as Design Element 1 (striped buds), Design Element 2 (brown abstract) and Design Element 3 (green and gold blobs on navy).

Template J: GP22GN only. Cut 2¹/₂in (6.5cm) wide strips along the length of the fabric. Cut 25 in Design Element 1, 35 in Design Element 2 and 30 in Design Element 3.

Template J: All other fabrics. Cut 2¹/₂in (6.5cm) wide strips across the width of the fabric. Each strip will give you 17 patches per 45in (114cm) wide fabric. Cut 41 in GP01R, 37 in GP25BK, 34 in GP26CR, 33 in GP08MG, 30 in GP24DE, 27 in GP23GD, 26 in BKC03, 25 in GP01G, GP01J, GP23BL, GP23BR, GP24LV, GP31BL, BKC02, BKC06, 24 in GP01L, 21 in GP20PN, 18 in DIP03 and 17 in GP32AN.

Borders: Cut 2 strips 8in x 61¹/₂in (20.5cm x 156cm) and 2 strips 8in x 52¹/₂in (20.5cm x 133.5cm) along the length of the fabric in GP31AN

Binding: Cut 7⅝yds (7m) of 2½in (6.5cm) wide bias binding in AWS01.

Backing: Cut 1 piece 44in x 68in (112cm x 173cm) and 1 piece 31in x 68in (79cm x 173cm) in backing fabric.

MAKING THE QUILT
Using a ¼in (6mm) seam allowance throughout, piece the template J squares into 26 rows of 23 squares. Refer to the quilt assembly diagram for fabric arrangement.

ADDING THE BORDERS
Add the borders to the quilt centre in the order indicated by the quilt assembly diagram.

FINISHING THE QUILT
Press the quilt top. Seam the backing pieces using a ¼in (6mm) seam allowance to form a piece approx. 74in x 68in (188cm x 173cm). Layer the quilt top, batting and backing and baste together (see page 120). Using dark red machine quilting thread, quilt the centre of the quilt as shown in the quilting diagram, this pattern defines the crosses to the best effect. Quilt the border in a meander style, emphasizing the flowers in the Zinnia fabric. Trim the quilt edges and attach the binding (see page 121).

Quilting Diagram

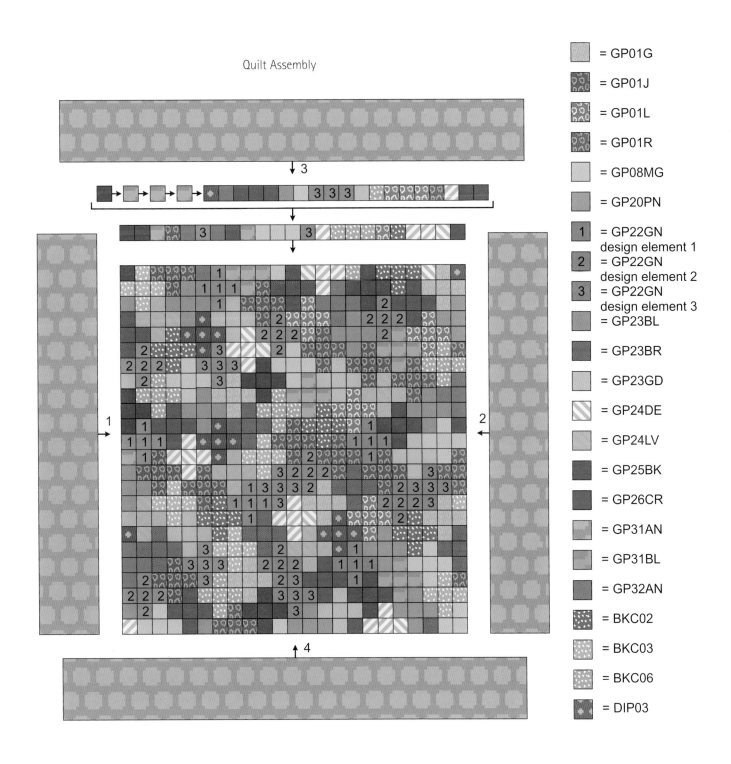

Quilt Assembly

= GP01G
= GP01J
= GP01L
= GP01R
= GP08MG
= GP20PN
1 = GP22GN design element 1
2 = GP22GN design element 2
3 = GP22GN design element 3
= GP23BL
= GP23BR
= GP23GD
= GP24DE
= GP24LV
= GP25BK
= GP26CR
= GP31AN
= GP31BL
= GP32AN
= BKC02
= BKC03
= BKC06
= DIP03

Currents Quilt ★★

KAFFE FASSETT

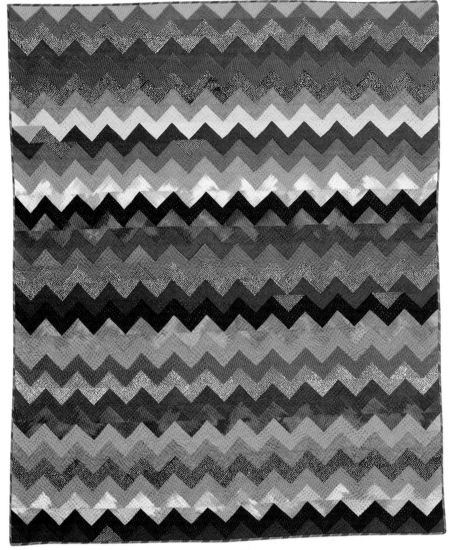

A classic zig-zag, this form always gets my attention, in textiles, architecture or graphics. I enjoyed for once playing with plainer shot cottons and my ikats from India, they show up the hand quilting well.

SIZE OF QUILT
The finished quilt will measure approx.
71¹/₂in x 85¹/₄in (181.5cm x 216.5cm).

MATERIALS
Patchwork Fabrics:
BATIK CONFETTI

Tomato	BKC01:	¹/₈yd (15cm)
Blue	BKC02:	⁵/₈yd (60cm)
Moss	BKC03:	³/₈yd (35cm)
Lilac	BKC06:	⁵/₈yd (60cm)

SINGLE IKAT WASH

Banana	SIW03:	³/₈yd (35cm)
Green	SIW04:	⁵/₈yd (60cm)
Red	SIW06:	⁵/₈yd (60cm)

SHOT COTTON

Chartreuse	SC12:	³/₈yd (35cm)
Sage	SC17:	⁵/₈yd (60cm)
Pine	SC21:	⁷/₈yd (80cm)
Watermelon	SC33:	⁵/₈yd (60cm)
Apple	SC39:	³/₈yd (35cm)
Jade	SC41:	⁷/₈yd (80cm)
Lime	SC43:	¹/₂yd (45cm)
Scarlet	SC44:	³/₄yd (70cm)
Grape	SC47:	⁷/₈yd (80cm)
Forget-Me-Not	SC51:	⁵/₈yd (60cm)

Backing Fabric:
Note: The backing for this quilt was pieced from the fabrics listed below, alternatively use 5¹/₄yds (4.8m) of any one of the fabrics.
EXOTIC STRIPE

	ES21: ³/₄yd (70cm)

NARROW STRIPE

	NS01: ³/₄yd (70cm)
	NS17: ³/₄yd (70cm)

PACHRANGI STRIPE

	PS13: ³/₄yd (70cm)
	PS05: ³/₄yd (70cm)

SINGLE IKAT FEATHERS

Curry	SIF01:	³/₄yd (70cm)
Earth	SIF02:	³/₄yd (70cm)
Raspberry	SIF06:	³/₄yd (70cm)

Binding:
AWNING STRIPE

Lilac	AWS04: ⁵/₈yd (60cm)

Batting:
80in x 92in (203cm x 234cm).

Quilting thread:
Stranded embroidery thread in pink, green, yellow and blue.

Templates:
see page 102, 103.

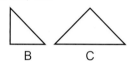

B   C

PATCH SHAPES
This quilt is made using 2 triangle patch shapes (Templates B & C). The larger triangle is pieced into rows with the smaller triangle used to fill in the ends of the rows. The rows are then joined to form the quilt.

CUTTING OUT
Template B: Cut 3⁵/₈in (9.25cm) wide strips across the width of the fabric. Cut 6 in SC21, SC41, SC44, SC47, 4 in BKC02, BKC06, SIW04, SIW06, SC17, SC33, SC51, 2 in BKC03, SIW03, SC12, SC39 and SC43. Reserve the remaining strips, trim and use for template C.
Template C: Cut 3³/₈in (8.5cm) wide strips across the width of the fabric. Each strip will give you 11 patches per 45in (114cm) wide fabric. Cut 75 in SC21, SC41, SC47, 56 in SC44, 50 in BKC02, BKC06, SIW04, SIW06, SC17, SC33, SC51, 39 in SC43, 25 in BKC03, SIW03, SC12, 24 in SC39 and 6 in BKC01.

Binding: Cut 9 yds (8.2m) of 2¹/₂in (6.5cm) wide bias binding in AWS06.

Backing:
For single fabric backing cut 1 piece 44in x 92in (112cm x 234cm) and 1 piece 37in x 92in (94cm x 234cm) in backing fabric.

For pieced backing cut 1 piece 12in x 44in (30.5cm x 112cm) and 1 piece 12in x 37in (30.5cm x 94cm) in ES21, NS01, NS17, PS05, PS13, SIF01, SIF02 and SIF06.

MAKING THE QUILT

Use a 1/4in (6mm) seam allowance throughout and refer to the quilt assembly diagram for fabric arrangement. Piece a total of 31 rows, each row has 25

template C triangles and 2 Template B triangles for the row ends. Join the rows to form the quilt.

FINISHING THE QUILT

Press the quilt top. For single fabric backing seam the 2 backing pieces using a 1/4in (6mm) seam allowance to form a piece approx. 80in x 92in (203cm x 234cm). For pieced backing join the 2

pieces of each fabric to form a long strip. In the order indicated in the backing diagram join the strips, staggering the seams as shown. Layer the quilt top, batting and backing and baste together (see page 120). Hand quilt in a geometric pattern as shown in the quilting diagram using stranded embroidery threads in pink, green, yellow and blue. Trim the quilt edges and attach the binding (see page 121).

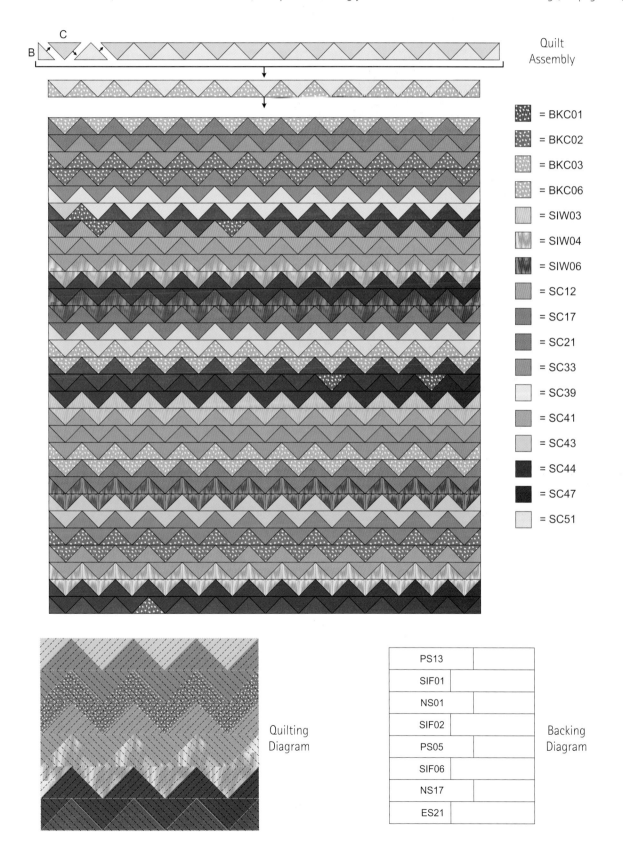

Quilt Assembly

= BKC01
= BKC02
= BKC03
= BKC06
= SIW03
= SIW04
= SIW06
= SC12
= SC17
= SC21
= SC33
= SC39
= SC41
= SC43
= SC44
= SC47
= SC51

Quilting Diagram

PS13	
SIF01	
NS01	
SIF02	
PS05	
SIF06	
NS17	
ES21	

Backing Diagram

En Kopp Te Til Kaffe Quilt ★ ★ ★
A Cup of Tea for Kaffe
HILDE AANERUD KROHG

Inspired by Kaffe's 'Rice Bowls' quilt Hilde has enjoyed using his smaller prints in this charming quilt.

Pastel	GP20PT:	¹/₈yd (15cm)
Sludge	GP20SL:	¹/₈yd (15cm)
PANSY		
Grey	GP23GY:	¹/₈yd (15cm)
KASHMIR		
Aqua	GP25AQ:	¹/₈yd (15cm)
Black	GP25BK:	¹/₈yd (15cm)
Grey	GP25GY:	¹/₂yd (45cm)
		includes binding.
Old Gold	GP25OG:	¹/₈yd (15cm)
WILD ROSE		
Lavender	GP26LV:	¹/₈yd (15cm)
Ochre	GP26OC:	¹/₈yd (15cm)
Peach	GP26PH:	¹/₈yd (15cm)
SHOT COTTON		
Opal	SC05:	¹/₈yd (15cm)
Bittersweet	SC10:	¹/₈yd (15cm)
Charcoal	SC25:	¹/₈yd (15cm)
Mist	SC48:	¹/₈yd (15cm)

Backing Fabric: 1⁵/₈yds (1.5m)
We suggest these fabrics for backing:
PAPERWEIGHT Sludge GP20SL
PANSY Grey GP23GY
WILD ROSE Ochre GP26OC

Binding:
KASHMIR
Grey GP25GY: see appliqué fabrics

Batting:
44in x 54in (112cm x 137cm).

Quilting thread:
Toning machine quilting threads.

Templates:
see page 111.

Rectangle

SIZE OF QUILT
The finished quilt will measure approx.
38¹/₂in x 48¹/₄in (98cm x 122.5cm).

MATERIALS
Patchwork Fabrics:
BATIK CONFETTI

Lilac	BKC06:	¹/₈yd (15cm)
OMBRE STRIPE		
	OS01:	⁵/₈yd (60cm)
WILD ROSE		
Pastel	GP26PT:	¹/₂yd (45cm)
SHOT COTTON		
Ginger	SC01:	¹/₄yd (25cm)
Cassis	SC02:	¹/₄yd (25cm)
Prune	SC03:	¹/₄yd (25cm)
Tangerine	SC11:	¹/₄yd (25cm)
Sage	SC17:	¹/₄yd (25cm)
Tobacco	SC18:	¹/₄yd (25cm)
Lichen	SC19:	¹/₄yd (25cm)
Smoky	SC20:	¹/₄yd (25cm)
Pewter	SC22:	¹/₄yd (25cm)
Ecru	SC24:	¹/₄yd (25cm)
Mushroom	SC31:	¹/₄yd (25cm)
Watermelon	SC33:	¹/₄yd (25cm)

Appliqué Fabrics
PAPERWEIGHT

Pumpkin	GP20PN:	¹/₈yd (15cm)

PATCH SHAPES
One rectangle shape cut to size is pieced into blocks for this quilt, each block then has an appliquéd cup and saucer, which is applied using fusible webbing. The blocks are interspaced with sashing strips and sashing posts. The blocks and sashing are then surrounded with a border with corner posts.

Quilt Assembly

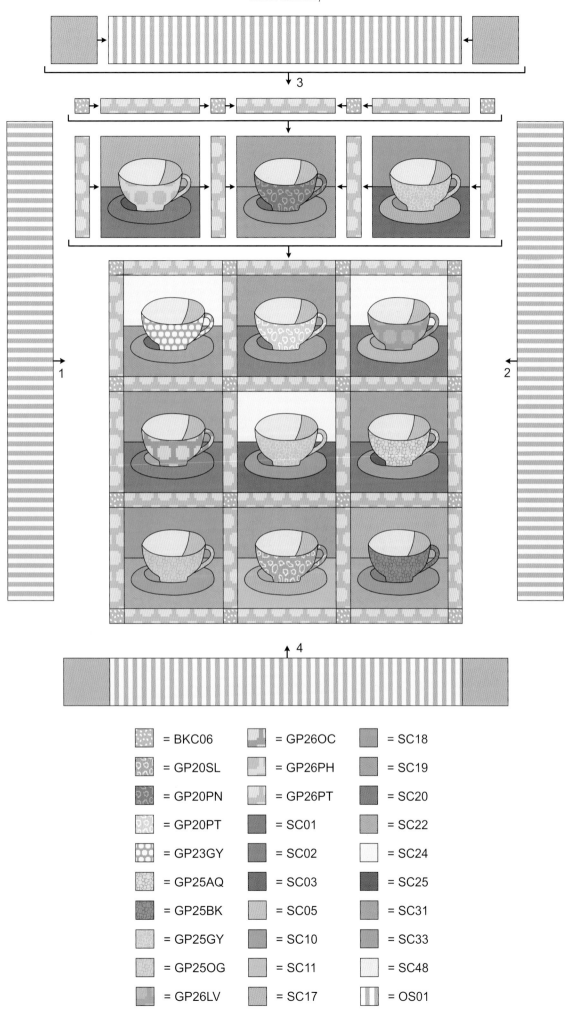

= BKC06	= GP26OC	= SC18
= GP20SL	= GP26PH	= SC19
= GP20PN	= GP26PT	= SC20
= GP20PT	= SC01	= SC22
= GP23GY	= SC02	= SC24
= GP25AQ	= SC03	= SC25
= GP25BK	= SC05	= SC31
= GP25GY	= SC10	= SC33
= GP25OG	= SC11	= SC48
= GP26LV	= SC17	= OS01

CUTTING OUT

Rectangle: Cut 4³/₄in (12cm) wide strips across the width of the fabric. From these cut rectangles 4³/₄in x 9in (12cmx 23cm), each strip will give you 4 rectangles. Cut 4 in SC31, 3 in SC01, SC24, 2 in SC03, SC17, SC18, SC19, SC22, 1 in SC02, SC11, SC20 and SC33. Reserve the remaining strip of SC17 fabric for Border Corner Posts.

Sashing Strips: Cut a total of 8 x 1³/₄in (4.5cm) wide strips across the width of the fabric. From these cut 31 sashing strips 1³/₄in x 9in (4.5cm x 23cm) in GP26PT.

Sashing Posts: Cut 1 x 1³/₄in (4.5cm) wide strip across the width of the fabric. From this cut 20 square sashing posts 1³/₄in x 1³/₄in (4.5cm x 4.5cm) in BKC06.

Border Corner Posts: Trim the remaining strip from cutting the rectangles in SC17 to 4¹/₂in (11.5cm) wide and cut 4 square sashing posts 4¹/₂in x 4¹/₂in (11.5cm x 11.5cm) in SC17.

Border: Cut 4 x 4¹/₂in (4.5cm) wide strips across the width of the fabric. From these cut 2 strips 4¹/₂in x 40³/₄in (11.5cm x 103.5cm) and 2 strips 4¹/₂in x 31in (11.5cm x 78.75cm) in OS 01.

Appliqué Shapes

Note: Usually when using fusible webbing the reversed appliqué shapes (we have provided reversed shapes for ease) are traced onto the webbing paper, then cut out roughly. The shapes do not need a seam allowance. The webbing shapes are then fused to the reverse of the fabrics and cut accurately. Follow the directions that come with the product you purchase.

Cups and Handles: Cut 2 sets in GP25GY, 1 set in GP20PN, GP20PT, GP20SL, GP23GY, GP25AQ, GP25BK, GP25OG, GP26LV, GP26OC and GP26PH.

Saucers: Cut 3 in SC10, 2 in SC17, SC19, 1 in SC02, SC11, SC20, SC31 and SC33.

Saucer Shadows: Cut 3 in SC22, 2 in SC02, SC03, SC10, SC25 and 1 in SC20.

Inside Cup: Cut 12 in SC48.

Inside Cup Shadow: Cut 12 in SC05.

Binding: Cut 5 strips 2¹/₂in (6.5cm) wide x width of fabric in GP25GY.

Backing: Cut 1 piece 44in x 54in (112cm x 137cm) in backing fabric.

MAKING THE BLOCKS

Use a ¹/₄in (6mm) seam allowance throughout and refer to the quilt assembly diagram for fabric arrangement. Piece a total of 12 blocks as shown in the block assembly diagram. Find the centre of each block and mark with a pencil dot. Trace the appliqué positioning guide (see page 112) onto a sheet of clear plastic. This will allow you to position the appliqué shapes accurately. The black dot on the guide is the centre of the block. Prepare all the appliqué shapes according to the instructions with your fusible webbing.

APPLIQUÉ INSTRUCTIONS

First take the inside cup shapes. The inside cup shape has an underlap and the inside cup shadow has a seam allowance. Turn under the seam allowance and then top stitch using a fine running stitch to the underlap of the inside cup shape. Make 12. Next arrange the appliqué shapes and fuse into place using the guide to position the shapes accurately. Pay careful attention to the manufacturers instructions on iron temperature. Blanket stitch the edges of the appliqué shapes by hand as Hilde has or machine stitch using a running or blanket stitch as shown in the photograph on page 33. Complete all 12 blocks.

ASSEMBLING THE QUILT

Piece the blocks into 4 rows of 3 blocks, interspacing with sashing strips and posts as shown in the quilt assembly diagram. Join the borders in the order indicated.

FINISHING THE QUILT

Press the quilt top. Layer the quilt top, batting and backing and baste together (see page 120). Machine quilt around each cup and saucer using matching thread, and quilt the sashing ¹/₄in (6mm) in from the seams with toning thread. Make a template for the border quilting pattern (see page 113). The repeat for the quilt top and bottom is slightly different from the sides. Trace the pattern onto the borders and machine quilt. Trim the quilt edges and attach the binding (see page 121).

Block assembly diagram

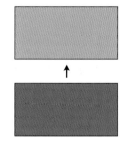

Floral Checkerboard Quilt ★ ★

KAFFE FASSETT

I was very pleased how my Lotus Leaf and Kimono fabric came out as prints so I wanted to show them to advantage. The checkerboard borders frame the large prints and keep the summer palette going.

Backing Fabric: 8⁷/₈yds (8.1m)
We suggest these fabrics for backing:
LOTUS LEAF Red GP29RD
ZINNIA Lime GP31LM
KIMONO Crimson/Magenta GP33CM
Leftover backing fabric can be used in the quilt.

Binding:
DIAGONAL POPPY
Duck Egg   GP24DE: ³/₄yd (70cm)

Batting:
104in x 104in (264cm x 264cm).

Quilting thread:
Toning machine quilting thread.

Templates:
see page 104.

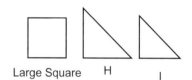

Large Square   H   I

PATCH SHAPES
A large square patch shape cut to size is pieced into diagonal rows separated by sashing strips. The edges and corners are completed using 2 triangle patch shapes (Templates H & I) The sashing strips are either pieced using the 'strip set' method (see below for details) or are cut from checkerboard fabrics. The quilt is then trimmed and framed with a double border. The templates for this quilt as printed at 50% of true size. Photocopy at 200% before using.

CUTTING OUT
Cut the fabric in the order stated. Note: The shapes for this quilt are large, therefore, to reduce waste, we suggest drawing round the templates for each patch shape onto the fabric for the best fit before cutting.
Inner Borders: Cut 2 strips 5¹/₂in x 91in (14cm x 231cm) and 2 strips 5¹/₂in x 81in (14cm x 206cm) along the length of the fabric in SIW04. Reserve the remaining fabric for sashing.

SIZE OF QUILT
The finished quilt will measure approx. 96¹/₂in x 96¹/₂in (245cm x 245cm).

MATERIALS
Main Patchwork Fabrics:
Lotus Leaf
Ochre   GP29OC: 1¹/₈yds (1m)
Red   GP29RD: 1¹/₂yds (1.4m)
Pastel   GP29PT: 1¹/₈yds (1m)
ZINNIA
Lime   GP31LM: ³/₈yd (35cm)
Magenta   GP31MG: ³/₈yd (35cm)
KIMONO
Crimson/Magenta GP33CM 1¹/₈yds (1m)
Sashing Fabrics:
PAPERWEIGHT
Lime   GP20LM: ³/₈yd (35cm)
PANSY
Mint   GP23MT: ¹/₄yd (25cm)
BATIK CONFETTI
Moss   BKC03: ¹/₂yd (45cm)

DOUBLE IKAT CHECKERBOARD
Magenta   DIC02: ¹/₂yd (45cm)
Gold   DIC04: ³/₈yd (35cm)
Swede   DIC05: ³/₈yd (35cm)
SINGLE IKAT WASH
Green   SIW04: ⁵/₈yd (60cm) or
                    use leftovers from borders
Red   SIW06: ³/₈yd (35cm)
SHOT COTTON
Ginger   SC01: ³/₈yd (35cm)
Bittersweet   SC10: ¹/₄yd (25cm)
Chartreuse   SC12: ³/₈yd (35cm)
Lavender   SC14: ¹/₂yd (45cm))
Mustard   SC16: ¹/₄yd (25cm)
Mushroom   SC31: ³/₈yd (35cm)
Jade   SC41: ¹/₄yd (25cm)
Border Fabrics
SINGLE IKAT WASH
Green   SIW04: 2⁵/₈yds (2.4m)
LEAVES
Jade   GP30JA: 1yd (90cm)

Strip Set 1

Strip Set 2

a

b

Quilt Assembly

Sashing

= GP29OC

= GP29RD

= GP29PT

= GP31LM

= GP31MG

= GP33CM

= SC01 & GP20LM

= SC31 & BKC03

= SC10 & BKC03

= SC16 & GP23MT

= SC14 & SIW06

= SC14 & SIW04

= SC12 & SIW04

= SC41 & SIW04

= DIC02

= DIC04

= DIC05

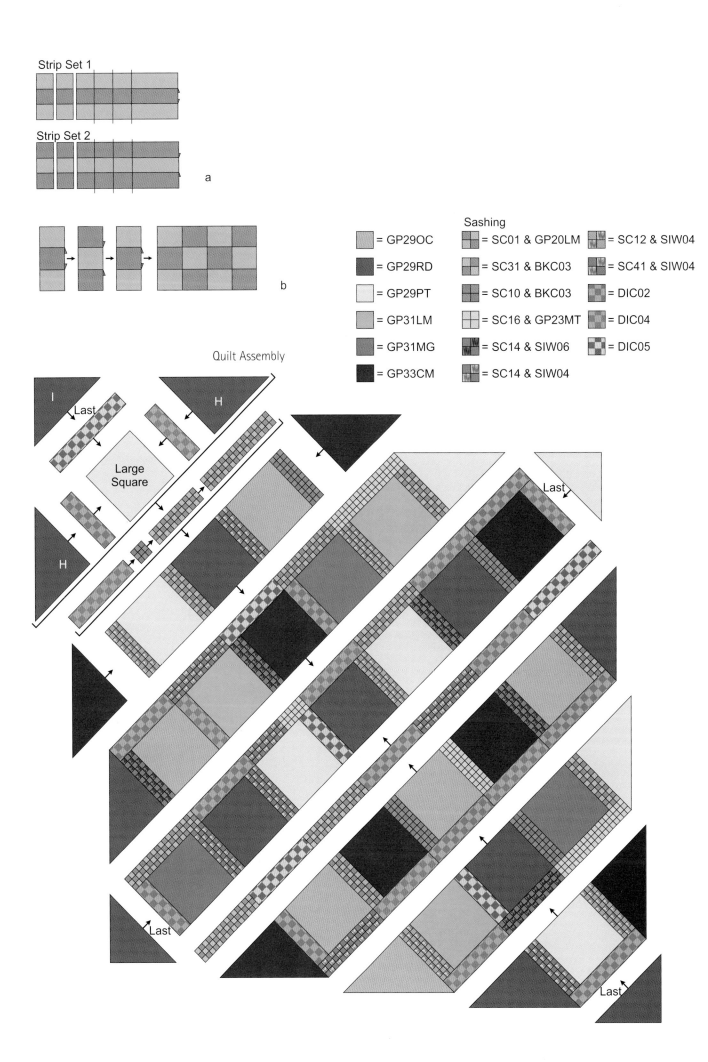

Outer Borders: Cut 9 strips 3¹/₂in (9cm) wide x width of fabric in GP30JA.

Large squares: Make a paper template 12¹/₂in (31.75cm) square. Cut 5 in GP29OC, GP29RD, GP29PT, 4 in GP33CM, 3 in GP31LM and GP31 MG.

Template H: Cut 5 in GP29RD, 4 in GP33CM, 2 in GP29PT and 1 in GP29OC.

Template I: Cut 3 in GP29RD and 1 in GP29PT.

Sashing:

Checkerboard Fabrics

Cut strips 3¹/₂in (9cm) wide x width of fabric, from these cut the following sashing strips:

18¹/₂in x 3¹/₂in (47cm x 9cm) Cut 2 in DIC02 and 2 in DIC05.

15¹/₂in x 3¹/₂in (39.5cm x 9cm) Cut 6 in DIC02, DIC04 and 2 in DIC05.

12¹/₂in x 3¹/₂in (31.75cm x 9cm) Cut 4 in DIC02 3 in DIC04 and 2 in DIC05.

Other Sashing Fabrics:

Cut strips 1¹/₂in (3.75cm) wide x width of fabric, for SIW04 cut 1¹/₂in x 44in (3.75cm x 112cm) strips down the length of the fabric if using leftover from borders.

Cut 12 in SIW04, 9 in BKC03, SC14, 6 in GP20LM, SIW06, SC01, SC12, SC31, 3 in GP23MT, SC10, SC16 and SC41.

Binding: Cut 10 strips 2¹/₂in (6.5cm) wide x width of fabric in GP24DE.

Backing: Cut 2 pieces 44in x 104in (112cm x 264cm) and 1 piece 17in x 104in (43cm x 264cm) in backing fabric.

MAKING THE PIECED SASHING

Using a ¹/₄in (6mm) seam allowance throughout, piece the 'Other Sashing Fabrics' into strip sets as shown in diagram a referring to the quilt assembly diagram and fabric key for fabric combinations. Press the seam allowances in opposite directions for each strip set as shown. Cut the strip sets into 1¹/₂in (3.75cm) slices. Alternate the slices from each strip set to create checkerboard sashing sections as shown in diagram b. In some cases 2 fabric combinations are used in 1 sashing section to avoid waste.

MAKING THE QUILT CENTRE

Lay out the large squares with the pieced and cut sashing sections, fill in the edges and corners with the template H & I triangles. Join into diagonal rows as shown in the quilt assembly diagram. Mark the quilt top as shown in the

trimming diagram and trim the quilt ensuring you leave a ¹/₄in (6mm) seam allowance outside the marked line.

ADDING THE BORDERS

Add the inner borders to the trimmed quilt centre in the order indicated by the quilt assembly diagram. For the outer borders join the strips as necessary and cut 2 side borders 3¹/₂in x 91in (9cm x 231cm) and 2 end borders 3¹/₂in x 97in (9cm x 246.5cm). Add these to the quilt in the order indicated by the quilt assembly diagram.

FINISHING THE QUILT

Press the quilt top. Seam the backing pieces using a ¹/₄in (6mm) seam allowance to form a piece approx.104in x 104in (264cm x 264cm). Layer the quilt top, batting and backing and baste together (see page 120). Using a toning machine quilting thread, quilt in the ditch along all the sashings and 2¹/₂in from the outside of each square and edge triangle, finally quilt a loose meander along the sashing. Trim the quilt edges and attach the binding (see page 121).

Trimming Diagram

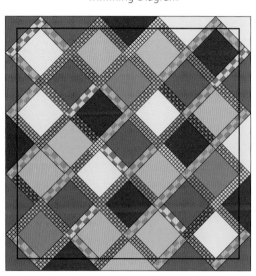

Quilt Assembly

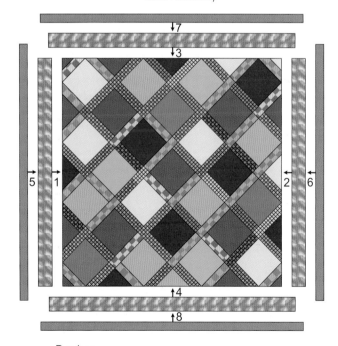

Borders

■ = GP30JA

▨ = SIW04

Rose Cottage Quilt ★ ★

ROBERTA HORTON

A vision straight out of a small village, or at least it seems so to an American who is a lover of British television period dramas. Roberta is ready to move into one of these cottages, complete with its English country garden.

SIZE OF QUILT
The finished quilt will measure approx. 65in x 78in (165cm x 198cm).

MATERIALS
Patchwork Fabrics:
WILD ROSE
Crimson	GP26CR:	1³/8yd (1.3m)
Lavender	GP26LV:	³/8yd (35cm)
Ochre	GP26OC:	³/8yd (35cm)
Peach	GP26PH:	³/8yd (35cm)
Pastel	GP26PT:	³/8yd (35cm)

LEAVES
Black	GP30BK:	³/4yd (70cm)
Blue	GP30BL:	7/8yd (80cm)
Jade	GP30JA:	³/8yd (35cm)
Ochre	GP30OC:	1/8yd (15cm)
Periwinkle	GP30PE:	1/2yd (45cm)

PAISLEY STRIPE
Antique	GP32AN:	1/4yd (25cm)
Blue	GP32BL:	1/4yd (25cm)
Bright	GP32BR:	1/4yd (25cm)
Red	GP32RD:	1/4yd (25cm)

Backing Fabric: 4¹/4yds (3.9m)
We suggest these fabrics for backing:
KASHMIR Black GP25BK
LEAVES Black GP30BK
WILD ROSE Ochre GP26OC

Binding:
LEAVES
Red	GP30RD:	5/8yd (60cm)

Batting:
72in x 85in (183cm x 216cm).

Quilting thread:
Invisible and red machine quilting thread.

Templates:
see page 103, 107, 108.

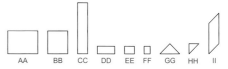

PATCH SHAPES
The cottage blocks are pieced using 3 large rectangle patch shapes (Templates AA, BB & CC), 3 small rectangle patch shapes (Templates DD, EE & FF), 2 triangle patch shapes (Templates GG & HH) and 1 lozenge patch shape (Template II) for the roof. The blocks are interspaced with sashing strips and posts. The quilt is finished with 2 simple borders.

CUTTING OUT
Template AA: Cut 5in (12.75cm) wide strips across the width of the fabric. Cut 6 in GP26LV, GP26PT, 4 in GP26OC and GP26PH. Reserve leftover strip for template BB.

Template BB: Cut 5in (12.75cm) wide strips across the width of the fabric. Cut 6 in GP26OC, GP26PH, 4 in GP26LV and GP26PT. Reserve leftover strip and trim for template GG.

Template CC: Cut 2¹/2in (6.5cm) wide strips across the width of the fabric. Each strip will give you 4 patches per 45in (114cm) wide fabric. Cut 20 in GP30JA.

Template DD: Cut 2in (5cm) wide strips across the width of the fabric. Each strip will give you 10 patches per 45in (114cm) wide fabric. Cut 20 in GP30PE.

Template EE: Cut 2in (5cm) wide strips across the width of the fabric. Each strip will give you 16 patches per 45in (114cm) wide fabric. Cut 40 in GP30PE.

Template FF: Cut 2in (5cm) wide strips across the width of the fabric. Each strip will give you 24 patches per 45in (114cm) wide fabric. Cut 40 in GP30OC.

Template GG: Cut 2⁵/8 in (6.75cm) wide strips across the width of the fabric. Cut 6 in GP26LV, GP26OC, 4 in GP26PH and GP26PT.

Template HH: Cut 2⁷/8in (7.5cm) wide

Quilt Assembly

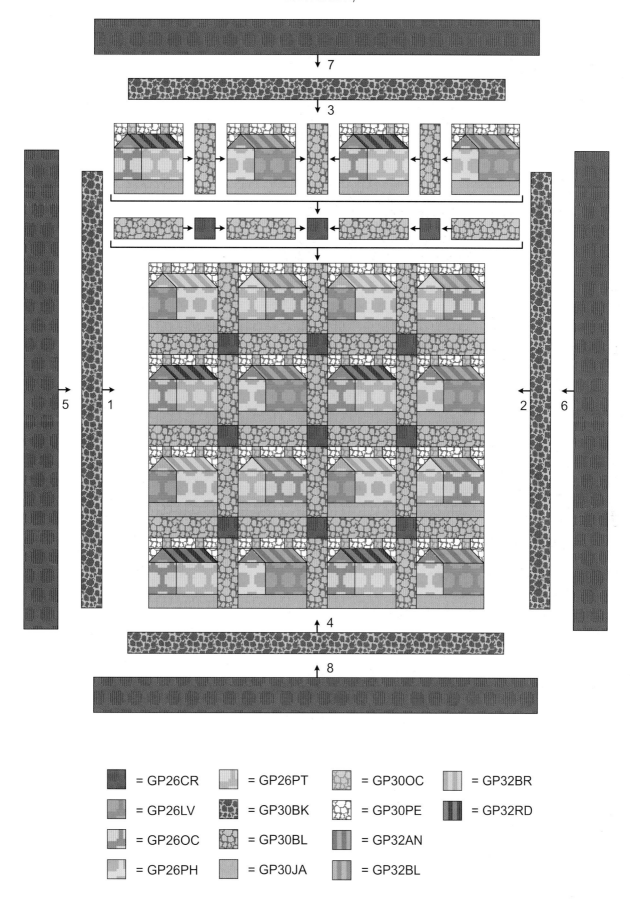

= GP26CR   = GP26PT   = GP30OC   = GP32BR

= GP26LV   = GP30BK   = GP30PE   = GP32RD

= GP26OC   = GP30BL   = GP32AN

= GP26PH   = GP30JA   = GP32BL

strips across the width of the fabric. Each strip will give you 28 patches per 45in (114cm) wide fabric. Cut 40 in GP30PE.
Template II: Cut 8³/₈in (21.25cm) wide strips across the width of the fabric. Cut 6 in GP32AN, GP32RD, 4 in GP32BL and GP32BR. The stripe direction is important, see the Template II Cutting Diagram below.
Sashing Strips: Cut a total of 8 x 3¹/₂in (9cm) wide strips across the width of the fabric. From these cut 31 sashing strips 3¹/₂in x 10¹/₂in (9cm x 26.75cm) in GP30BL.
Sashing Posts: Cut 1 x 3¹/₂in (9cm) wide strip across the width of the fabric. From this cut 12 square sashing posts 3¹/₂in x 3¹/₂in (9cm x 9cm) in GP26CR.
Inner Border: Cut 6 strips 3¹/₂in (9cm) x the width of the fabric, join as necessary. Cut 2 strips 3¹/₂in x 62¹/₂in (9cm x 158.75cm) and 2 strips 3¹/₂in x 55¹/₂in (9cm x 141cm) in GP30BK.
Outer Border: Cut 7 strips 5¹/₂in (14cm) x

the width of the fabric, join as necessary. Cut 2 strips 5¹/₂in x 68¹/₂in (14cm x 174cm) and 2 strips 5¹/₂in x 65¹/₂in (14cm x 166.5cm) in GP26CR.

Binding: Cut 7 strips 2¹/₂in (6.5cm) wide x width of fabric in GP30RD.

Backing: Cut 1 piece 44in x 72in (112cm x 183cm) and 1 piece 42in x 72in (107cm x 183cm) in backing fabric.

MAKING THE BLOCKS
Use a ¹/₄in (6mm) seam allowance throughout. Following the block assembly diagram and referring to the Block Diagram for fabric combinations make 6 each of blocks A and B, and 4 each of blocks C and D.

MAKING THE QUILT
Lay out the blocks as shown in the quilt assembly diagram interspacing the blocks with sashing strips and posts as shown.

Join the bocks and sashing into rows and then join the rows to form the quilt centre. Finally add the inner and outer borders in the order indicated.

FINISHING THE QUILT
Press the quilt top. Seam the backing pieces using a ¹/₄in (6mm) seam allowance to form a piece approx. 72in x 85in (183cm x 216cm). Layer the quilt top, batting and backing and baste together (see page 120). Machine quilt as shown in the quilting diagram, using invisible machine quilting thread for the sashing seams, the house seams and to meander quilt the sky and ground sections. Use black quilting thread to echo the fabric stripes on the roof sections and to add a door and windows to each block. Use red quilting thread for the sashings and borders. Trim the quilt edges and attach the binding (see page 121).

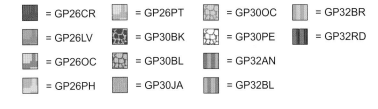

= GP26CR	= GP26PT	= GP30OC	= GP32BR
= GP26LV	= GP30BK	= GP30PE	= GP32RD
= GP26OC	= GP30BL	= GP32AN	
= GP26PH	= GP30JA	= GP32BL	

Block Diagram

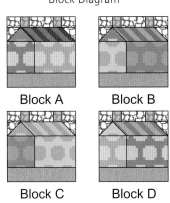

Block A   Block B

Block C   Block D

Block Assembly Diagram

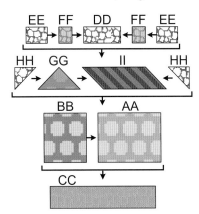

EE FF DD FF EE

HH GG II HH

BB AA

CC

Quilting Diagram

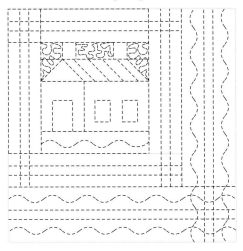

Template II Cutting Diagram

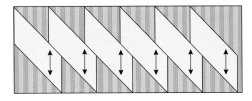

My Fair Lady Quilt ★★

BRANDON MABLY

Repetition of any form gives me great pleasure, indeed flipping through an old book on stripy quilts this 'spider web' layout put me in mind of the parasols at the horse race in the film 'My Fair Lady'. Slate Batik Confetti fabric is a pleasing background for the soft calm prints of the blocks.

SIZE OF QUILT
The finished quilt will measure approx.
70³/₄in x 81¹/₂in (180cm x 207cm).

MATERIALS
Patchwork Fabrics:
BATIK CONFETTI
Slate   BKC04: 2¹/₄yds (2.1m)
BLUE & WHITE STRIPE
                     BWS01: ³/₈yd (35cm)
                     BWS02: ³/₈yd (35cm)
PAPERWEIGHT
Pumpkin   GP20PN: ¹/₄yd (25cm)
Pastel   GP20PT: ³/₈yd (35cm)
Sludge   GP20SL: ³/₈yd (35cm)
PANSY
Grey   GP23GY: ³/₈yd (35cm)
Mint   GP23MT: ³/₈yd (35cm)
DIAGONAL POPPY
Pink   GP24PK: ³/₈yd (35cm)

KASHMIR
Aqua   GP25AQ: ¹/₂yd (45cm)
Black   GP25BK: ³/₈yd (35cm)
Blue   GP25BL: ³/₈yd (35cm)
Grey   GP25GY: ¹/₂yd (45cm)
Raspberry   GP25RS: ¹/₄yd (25cm)
WILD ROSE
Lavender   GP26LV: ¹/₈yd (15cm)
Ochre   GP26OC: ¹/₄yd (25cm)
Pastel   GP26PT: ¹/₄yd (25cm)
PAISLEY STRIPE
Misty   GP32MS: ³/₈yd (35cm)

Backing Fabric: 4¹/₂yds (4.1m)
We suggest these fabrics for backing:
WILD ROSE Ochre GP26OC or Pastel
GP26PT
PAISLEY STRIPE Misty GP32MS

Binding:
DIAGONAL POPPY
Duck Egg   GP24DE: ⁵/₈yd (60cm)

Batting:
79in x 88in (201cm x 224cm).

Quilting thread:
Toning machine quilting thread and hand quilting thread.

Templates:
see page 105.

PATCH SHAPES
Strip sets of 2 narrow and 1 wide fabric strips are joined and then cut to an equilateral triangle shape (Template Y). The triangles are then pieced into hexagonal blocks, each strip set yields 2 different blocks, (see block assembly diagram c). The blocks are joined into rows along with additional background triangles cut from template Y. A second triangle shape (Template Z) is used to complete the quilt top and bottom. Note: The fabric Brandon chose for the background of this quilt (BKC04) is reversible, if you choose a non reversible fabric you will need to make an additional 'reverse' template for shape Z.

Quilt Assembly

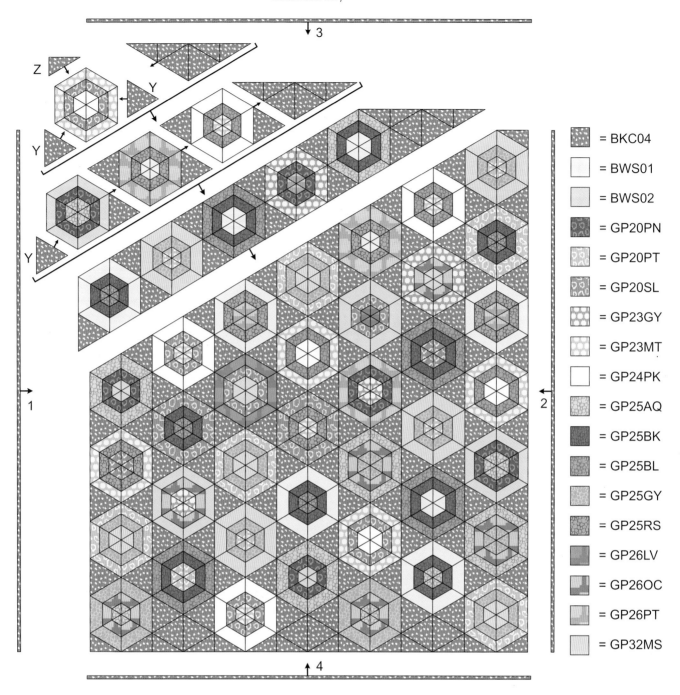

▨	= BKC04
☐	= BWS01
▨	= BWS02
▨	= GP20PN
▨	= GP20PT
▨	= GP20SL
▨	= GP23GY
▨	= GP23MT
☐	= GP24PK
▨	= GP25AQ
▨	= GP25BK
▨	= GP25BL
▨	= GP25GY
▨	= GP25RS
▨	= GP26LV
▨	= GP26OC
▨	= GP26PT
▨	= GP32MS

Quilting Diagram

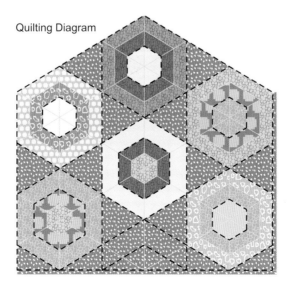

72

CUTTING OUT

Template Y: Background fabric BKC04 only.

Cut 5³/₄in (14.75cm) wide strips across the width of the fabric. Each strip will give you 11 patches per 45in (114cm) wide fabric. Cut 102.

Template Z: Background fabric BKC04 only. Cut 3¹/₂in (9cm) wide strips across the width of the fabric. Each strip will give you 12 patches per 45in (114cm) wide fabric. Cut 28.

Borders: Cut 8 strips 1in (2.5cm) x the width of the fabric, join as necessary and cut 2 strips 1in x 82in (2.5cm x 208.25cm) and 2 strips 1in x 72¹/₂ in (2.5cm x 184cm) in BKC04, these borders are generous, trim to fit exactly.

Strip Set Fabric: Cut 2³/₄in (7cm) wide strips across the width of the fabric. Cut 4 in GP24PK, GP32MS, 3 in BWS01, 2 in GP20SL, GP23GY, GP25AQ, GP25GY, GP26PT, 1 in BWS02 and GP20PT. Total 23 strips.
Cut 2in (5cm) wide strips across the width of the fabric. Cut 6 in GP25BL, 5 in GP23MT, GP25BK, 4 in GP20PT, GP25GY, 3 in BWS02, GP20PN, GP20SL, GP25AQ, GP25RS, GP26OC, 2 in BWS01, 1 in GP26LV and GP26PT. Total 46 strips.

Binding: Cut 8 strips 2¹/₂in (6.5cm) wide x width of fabric in GP24DE.
Backing: Cut 2 pieces 44in x 79in (112cm x 201cm) in backing fabric.

MAKING THE BLOCKS

Use a ¹/₄in (6mm) seam allowance throughout. First sort all the fabric strips into sets. Each set has 1 x 2³/₄in (7cm) wide strip and 2 x 2in (5mm) wide strips, there are enough strips for 23 sets. Each strip set will yield 2 blocks, Block A and Block B, which look very different (see block assembly diagram c). When sorting your fabric strips look for the blocks with the larger centre sections (Block A) to identify the fabric combinations.
Join the first strip set as shown in the cutting diagram, press carefully. Starting 1in (2.5cm) in from the end of the strip cut into equilateral triangles using Template Y. You will get 6 'A' triangles and 5 'B' triangles. Take the 2 end pieces of the strip, join as shown and cut a 6th 'B' triangle, centring the seam. Take the 6 'A' triangles and join to form Block A following diagrams a and b. Next take the 6 'B' triangles and join in the same way

to form Block B. Make the strip sets, cut and piece one at a time to prevent the triangles being mixed up. Make a total of 46 blocks (23 Block A and 23 Block B).

MAKING THE QUILT

Lay out the blocks as shown in the quilt assembly diagram filling the gaps with the background triangles. Along the top and bottom edges of the quilt there are 6 pieced background sections. Join template Y and Z background triangles as shown in diagram d for these sections. Carefully separate the diagonal rows and join as shown in the quilt assembly diagram. Join the rows to form the quilt

centre. Finally trim the borders to fit and add in the order indicated.

FINISHING THE QUILT

Press the quilt top. Seam the backing pieces using a ¹/₄in (6mm) seam allowance to form a piece approx. 79in x 88in (201cm x 224cm). Layer the quilt top, batting and backing and baste together (see page 120). Using a toning machine quilting thread, quilt-in-the-ditch around the hexagons and along the quilt top and bottom, as shown in the quilting diagram. Also, hand quilt around the seams in each block as shown. Trim the quilt edges and attach the binding (see page 121).

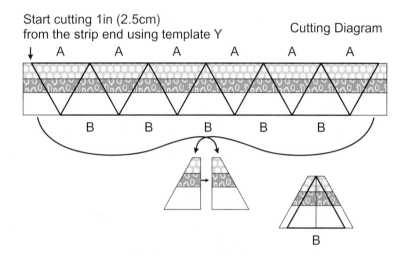

Start cutting 1in (2.5cm) from the strip end using template Y

Cutting Diagram

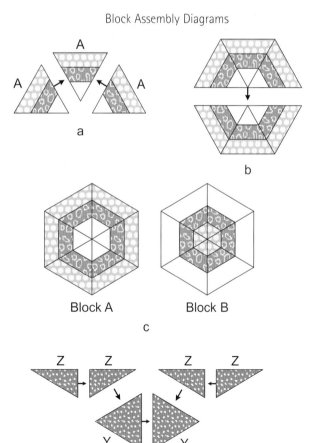

Block Assembly Diagrams

a

b

Block A   Block B

c

d

Light and Dark Checkerboard Quilt ★★

K A F F E   F A S S E T T

This is based on an old quilt I bought at a quilt fair in Holland. It was American and very monotone for me, but the effect of that central panel of slightly different tones haunted me. I have it on my bed now and it gives the room a strong sense of calm.

SIZE OF QUILT
The finished quilt will measure approx. 92in x 92in (233.5cm x 233.5cm).

MATERIALS
Patchwork Fabrics:
BATIK CONFETTI
Blue   BKC02: 1/2yd (45cm)
Slate   BKC04: 1 yd (90cm)
              includes binding.
Midnight   BKC05: 3 3/4yds (3.4m)
PEONY
Red   GP17RD: 1/2yd (45cm)
Taupe   GP17TA: 1/4yd (25cm)
OMBRE STRIPE
              OS05: 1/8yd (15cm)

Light Background Fabrics:
6 fabrics: 7/8yd (80cm) of each.
The following fabrics were included in this quilt, however any of the light Rowan prints would be suitable as they are used wrong side up for a very pale colourwash effect.
PEONY Violet GP17VI
PAPERWEIGHT Pastel GP20PT
DIAGONAL POPPY Pink GP24PK
WILD ROSE Pastel GP26PT
SHOT COTTON Blush SC28
SINGLE IKAT WASH Lavender SIW05

Backing Fabric: 8 5/8yds (7.9m)
We suggest these fabrics for backing:
BATIK CONFETTI Blue BKC02
PAPERWEIGHT Pastel GP20PT
WILD ROSE Pastel GP26PT
Leftover backing fabric can be used in the quilt.

Binding:
BATIK CONFETTI
Slate   BKC04:
              see patchwork fabrics.

Batting:
100in x 100in (254cm x 254cm).

Quilting thread:
Toning machine quilting thread.

Templates:
see page 102.

J

PATCH SHAPES
A single square patch shape (Template J) is used for this quilt. We have drawn an accurate diagram of the centre section, but the outer areas are a very simple dark (BKC05) and 'light' checkerboard. The 'light' background fabrics are all used wrong side up for an even paler effect. The whole quilt is 46 patches x 46 patches.

CUTTING OUT
Template J: Cut 2 1/2in (6.5cm) wide strips across the width of the fabric. Each strip will give you 17 patches per 45in (114cm) wide fabric. Cut 858 in BKC05, 81 in BKC02, GP17RD, 38 in BKC04, 30 in GP17TA and 8 in OS05. Also cut a total of 1020 patches in 'light' background fabrics. Total 2116 patches.

Binding: Cut 10 strips 2 1/2in (6.5cm) wide x width of fabric in BKC04.

Backing: Cut 2 pieces 44in x 100in (112cm x 254cm) and 1 piece 13in x 100in (33cm x 254cm) in backing fabric.

MAKING THE QUILT
Using a 1/4in (6mm) seam allowance throughout, piece the centre section as shown in the Quilt Centre diagram. If you have chosen different fabrics from our suggestions for the 'light' background fabrics substitute the ones you have chosen for the patches coloured as GP17VI, GP20PT, GO24PK, GP26PT, SC28 and SIW06. All the background fabrics are used wrong side up.

Next piece the checkerboard sections, ensure EVERY section has a dark (BKC05) square at the top left, this will ensure that the checkerboard pattern runs correctly across the whole quilt. Again, all the 'light' background fabrics are used wrong side up. Make up 4 sections 12 patches x 12 patches, as shown in diagram a, 2 sections 22 patches x 12 patches and 2 sections 12 patches x 22 patches. Piece the checkerboard sections together with the centre section as shown in Diagram b.

FINISHING THE QUILT
Press the quilt top. Seam the backing pieces using a 1/4in (6mm) seam allowance to form a piece approx. 100in x 100in (254cm x 254cm). Layer the quilt top, batting and backing and baste together (see page 120). Using toning machine quilting thread, quilt in the ditch. Trim the quilt edges and attach the binding (see page 121).

Diagram b

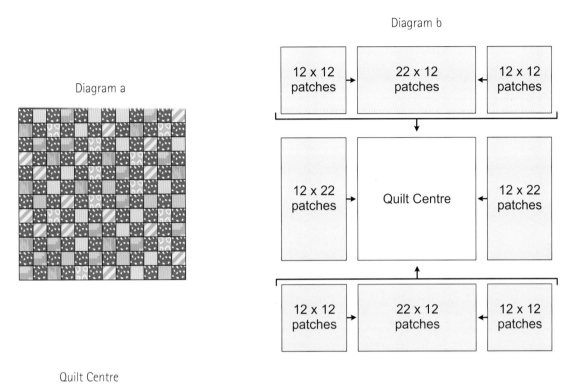

Diagram a

Quilt Centre

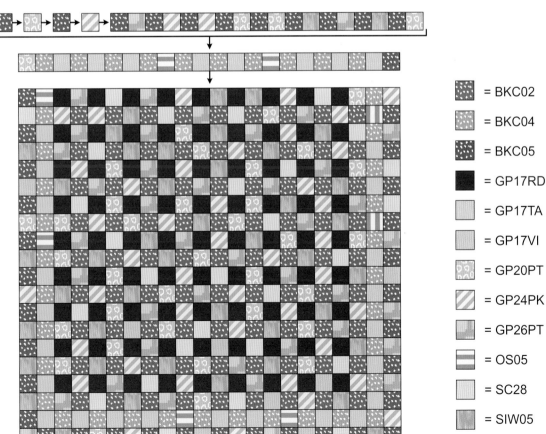

= BKC02

= BKC04

= BKC05

= GP17RD

= GP17TA

= GP17VI

= GP20PT

= GP24PK

= GP26PT

= OS05

= SC28

= SIW05

Parterre Quilt ★

PAULINE SMITH

A visit to a garden with formal flower beds divided by brick pathways sparked off this idea.

SIZE OF QUILT
The finished quilt will measure approx. 83in x 83in (211cm x 211cm).

MATERIALS
Patchwork Fabrics:
Peony
Maroon   GP17MR: ⁵/₈yd (60cm)
AUGUST ROSES
Purple   GP18PU: ³/₄yd (70cm)
SWIGGLE STRIPE
Pink   GP22PK: 2¹/₂yds (2.3m)
DIAGONAL POPPY
Aubergine   GP24AU: ⁵/₈yd (60cm)
KASHMIR
Grey   GP25GY: ¹/₂yd (45cm)
WILD ROSE
Crimson   GP26CR: 2¹/₂yds (2.3m)
                includes borders

SINGLE IKAT FEATHERS
Raspberry   SIF06: ⁵/₈yd (60cm)
SINGLE IKAT WASH
Red   SIW06: ⁵/₈yd (60cm)

Backing Fabric: 5¹/₄yds (4.8m)
We suggest these fabrics for backing:
WILD ROSE Crimson GP26CR
SINGLE IKAT FEATHERS Raspberry SIF06
SPOOLS Magenta GP34MG

Binding:
SWIGGLE STRIPE
Pink   GP22PK:
                see patchwork fabrics

Batting:
90in x 90in (229cm x 229cm).

Quilting thread:
Dark red machine quilting thread.

Templates:
see page 102.

A

PATCH SHAPES
A triangle patch shape (Template A) is pieced into blocks for the centre of this quilt. This is then framed with a simple border.

CUTTING OUT
Cut the fabric in the order stated.
Borders: Cut 2 strips 6in x 83¹/₂in (15.25cm x 212cm) and 2 strips 6in x 72¹/₂in (15.25cm x 184cm) along the length of the fabric in GP26CR. Reserve the remaining fabric for template A.

The Pink Swiggle Stripe fabric (GP22PK) has four distinct design elements. These have been separated and individually coloured in the quilt assembly diagram. Design Element 1 (striped buds) and Design Element 2 (pink swiggle on green) are used in the main quilt. Design Element 3 (stripes) is used for the binding.
Template A: GP22PK only. Cut 4⁷/₈in (12.5cm) wide strips along the length of the fabric. Cut 72 in Design Element 1 and 54 in Design Element 2.
Template A: All other fabrics. Cut 4⁷/₈in (12.5cm) wide strips across the width of the fabric. Each strip will give you 18 patches per 45in (114cm) wide fabric. Cut 90 in GP18PU, GP26CR, 72 in GP17MR, GP24AU (Note: for GP24AU cut the triangles so the stripes run parallel with the long side of the triangle), SIF06, SIW06, and 54 in GP25GY.

Binding: Cut 9³/₄yds (8.9m) of 2¹/₂in (6.5cm) wide binding in GP22PK Design Element 3.

Backing: Cut 2 pieces 45in x 90in (115cm x 229cm) in backing fabric.

MAKING THE QUILT
Using a ¹/₄in (6mm) seam allowance

throughout, piece a total of 9 blocks as shown in the block assembly diagram. Piece the blocks into 3 rows of 3 blocks then join the rows to form the quilt centre.

ADDING THE BORDERS
Add the borders to the quilt centre in the order indicated by the quilt assembly diagram.

FINISHING THE QUILT
Press the quilt top. Seam the backing pieces using a ¹/₄in (6mm) seam allowance to form a piece approx. 90in x 90in (229cm x 229cm). Layer the quilt top, batting and backing and baste together (see page 120). Using a dark red machine quilting thread, quilt a diagonal grid as shown in the quilting diagram. Trim the quilt edges and attach the binding (see page 121).

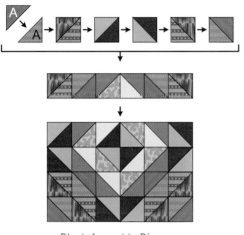

Block Assembly Diagram

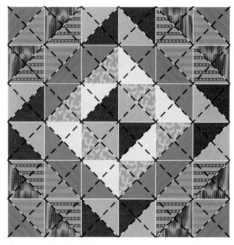

Quilting Diagram

Quilt Assembly

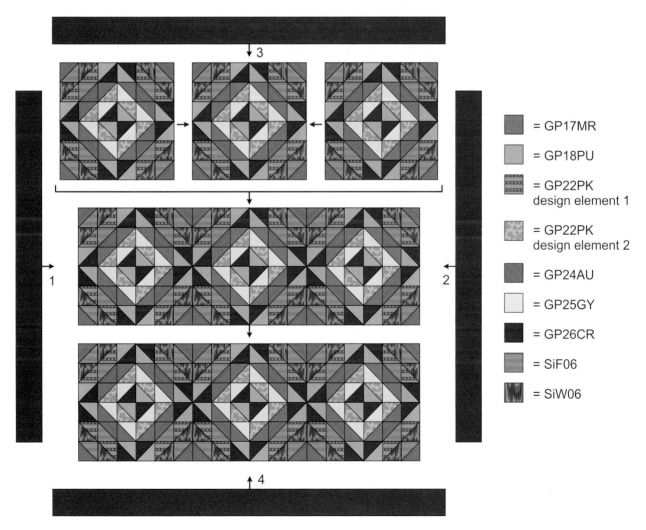

= GP17MR

= GP18PU

= GP22PK
design element 1

= GP22PK
design element 2

= GP24AU

= GP25GY

= GP26CR

= SiF06

= SiW06

Wallpaper Strips Quilt ★

KAFFE FASSETT

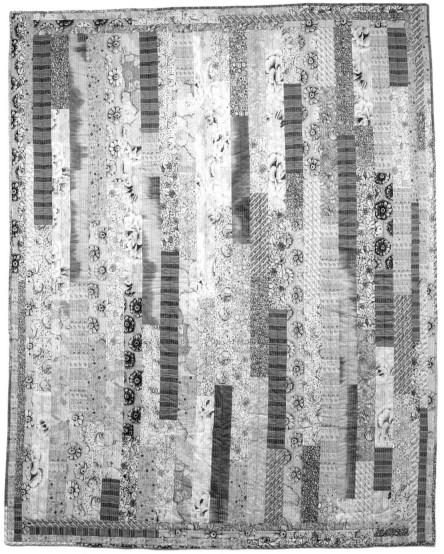

I don't know about you but I always fall in love with old houses in mid-restoration when stripping reveals past wallpapers and colours of the room. I picked the softest of my prints and reversed some to give that dusty, faded effect.

SIZE OF QUILT
The finished quilt will measure approx.
86in x 71in (218cm x 180cm).

MATERIALS
Patchwork Fabrics:
AWNING STRIPE
Orange   AWS02: ⁵/₈yd (60cm)
FORGET-ME-NOT ROSE
Blue/White   GP08BW: ⁵/₈yd (60cm)
PAPERWEIGHT
Pastel   GP20PT: ¹/₂yd (45cm)
DIAGONAL POPPY
Duck Egg   GP24DE: ³/₈yd (35cm)
Pink   GP24PK: ³/₈yd (35cm)

KASHMIR
Aqua   GP25AQ: ¹/₂yd (45cm)
Blue   GP25BL: ¹/₂yd (45cm)
WILD ROSE
Pastel   GP26PT: ¹/₂yd (45cm)
LOTUS LEAF
Pastel   GP29PT: ⁵/₈yd (60cm)
LEAVES
Periwinkle   GP30PE: ⁵/₈yd (60cm)
ZINNIA
Sky   GP31SK: ⁵/₈yd (60cm)
PAISLEY STRIPE
Misty   GP32MS: ¹/₂yd (45cm)
KIMONO
Lavender/Blue GP33LB: ¹/₂yd (45cm)

Pink/Orange   GP33PO: ¹/₂yd (45cm)
SINGLE IKAT WASH
Lavender   SIW05: ¹/₂yd (45cm)

Backing Fabric: 5³/₈yds (4.9m).
We suggest these fabrics for backing:
FORGET-ME-NOT ROSE
Blue/White   GP08BW
KASHMIR Blue   GP25BL
LOTUS LEAF Pastel GP29PT
Leftover backing fabric can be used in
the quilt.

Binding:
See patchwork fabrics

Batting:
93in x 78in (236cm x 198cm).

Quilting thread:
Toning hand quilting thread.

PATCH SHAPES
This quilt is pieced from strips cut from
the width of the fabric. The strips are cut
to random lengths and pieced into rows.
The rows are then joined to form the
quilt centre. The borders are made in a
similar way. Kaffe chose to reverse the
fabrics some of the time, this gives a
softer 'washed' look to the quilt and adds
variety using fewer fabrics.

CUTTING OUT
Cut a total of 45 x 3¹/₂in (9cm) wide
strips across the width of the fabric for
the quilt centre.
Cut a total of 25 x 1³/₄in (4.5cm) wide
strips across the width of the fabric for
the borders.

Binding: Cut 8 x 2¹/₂in (6.5cm) wide
strips across the width of the fabric. Cut
the strips into random lengths and piece
into a long strip 9yds (8.3m).

Backing: Cut 1 piece 44in x 93in (112cm
x 236cm) and 1 piece 35in x 93in (89cm x
236cm) in backing fabric.

MAKING THE QUILT CENTRE
Use a ¹/₄in (6mm) seam allowance
throughout. We have drawn Kaffe's quilt
accurately, however this quilt is intended
to be pieced fairly randomly. Take the
3¹/₂in (9cm) wide strips and cut into

random lengths. The lengths used in this quilt range from 7in (18cm) up to 42in (107cm). Piece the random lengths into 21 rows, each about 83in (210cm) long, the fabrics can be used either 'right' side or 'wrong' side facing up.

Lay the rows out, placing them so that the seams do not match, like brickwork. The top and bottom of the quilt will be trimmed, so don't worry about ragged edges at the top and bottom. Also try not to get 2 pieces of the same fabric next to each other. See diagram a. Join the rows together, stitching the first seam top to bottom, then the second bottom to top, carry on in this manner until all the rows are joined. This helps to prevent warping. Trim the quilt centre to 78¹/₂in (199.5cm), removing the ragged edges in the process as shown in diagram b.

MAKING THE BORDERS
Use the same method to piece the borders using the 1³/₄in (4.5cm) wide strips. Each border has 3 rows. Trim the top and bottom borders to 63¹/₂in (161cm) and the side borders to 86¹/₂in (220cm). Join the borders to the quilt centre in the order indicated in the quilt assembly diagram.

FINISHING THE QUILT
Press the quilt top. Seam the backing pieces using a ¹/₄in (6mm) seam allowance to form a piece approx. 93in x 78in (236cm x 198cm). Layer the quilt top, batting and backing and baste together (see page 120). Using toning hand quilting thread quilt a simple line along the centre of each row. Trim the quilt edges and attach the binding (see page 121).

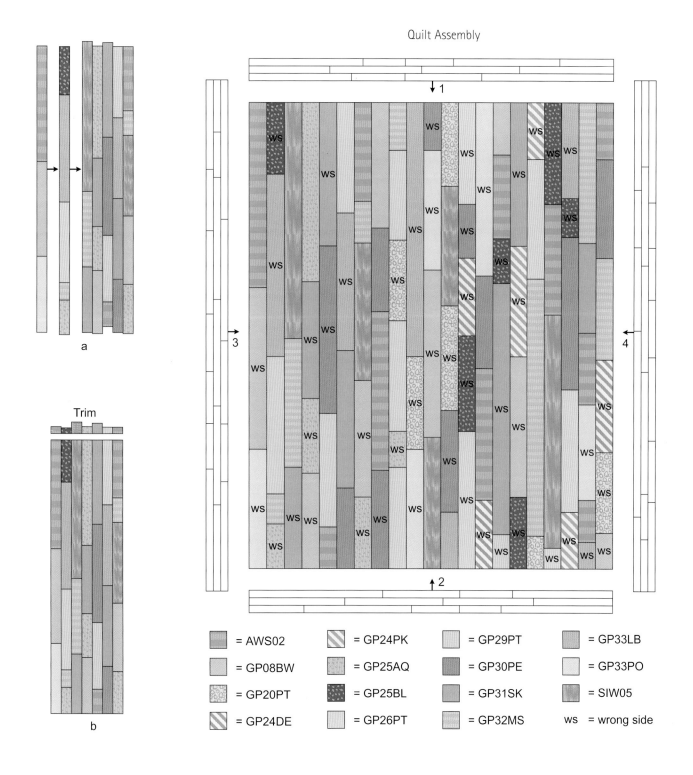

a

Trim

b

Quilt Assembly

	= AWS02		= GP24PK		= GP29PT		= GP33LB
	= GP08BW		= GP25AQ		= GP30PE		= GP33PO
	= GP20PT		= GP25BL		= GP31SK		= SIW05
	= GP24DE		= GP26PT		= GP32MS	ws	= wrong side

Romantic Rosy Quilt ★

LIZA PRIOR LUCY

Kaffe and Liza's first book, Glorious Patchwork, featured a quilt called Rosy. It was the first quilt they made together. Here comes Rosy again, this time in deep rich colours. The fabrics are from our newest collections. Some are designed by Kaffe, some by newcomer Martha Negley and some are from the Lille Collection of re-coloured vintage fabrics. This quilt is suitable for beginners as it is very simple to make. It is the colour and pattern that makes it appear complex.

SIZE OF QUILT
The finished quilt will measure approx. 60in x 78in (152.5cm x 198cm).

MATERIALS
Patchwork Fabrics:
LEAVES
Black   GP30BK: 1/4yd (25cm)
ZINNIA
Crimson   GP31CR: 1/2yd (45cm)

SPOOLS
Blue   GP34BL: 1/8yd (15cm)
Brown   GP34BR: 1/8yd (15cm)
Magenta   GP34MG: 1/4yd (25cm)
BEACHBALLS
Moody   GP37MO: 3/8yd (35cm)
FLOWER SPRAYS
Black   LC01BK: 3/8yd (35cm)
HYDRANGEA
Black   LC02BK: 3/8yd (35cm)

Tobacco   LC02TO: 1/2yd (45cm)
DOTTED LEAF
Azure   LC03AZ: 1/8yd (15cm)
Green   LC03GN: 1/8yd (15cm)
Periwinkle   LC03PE: 1/8yd (15cm)
NOSEGAY
Black   LC04BK: 1/2yd (45cm)
ARBOUR
Tobacco   LC05TO: 3/8yd (35cm)
TOSSED VEGETABLES
Dark   MN01DK: 3/8yd (35cm)
TWIG STRIPE
Dark   MN03DK: 1/4yd (25cm)
Red   MN03RD: 1/4yd (25cm)
VEGETABLE LEAVES
Dark   MN05DK: 3/8yd (35cm)
Red   MN05RD: 1/2yd (45cm)
SINGLE IKAT FEATHERS
Storm   SIF03: 5/8yd (60cm)
Raspberry   SIF06: 5/8yd (60cm)

Backing Fabric: 4 yds (3.6m)
We suggest these fabrics for backing:
SINGLE IKAT FEATHERS Raspberry SIF06
TWIG STRIPE Dark MN03DK
VEGETABLES LEAVES Dark MN05DK

Binding:
ROMAN GLASS
Jungle   GP01JG: 5/8yd (60cm)

Batting:
66in x 84in (168cm x 213.5cm).

Quilting thread:
Dark red machine quilting thread.

Templates:
see page 109.

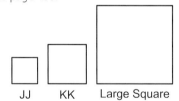

JJ   KK   Large Square

PATCH SHAPES
Nine-patch blocks are pieced from a small square patch shape (Template JJ), these are alternated with large squares, cut to size, and are joined into rows. The rows are joined to form the quilt centre. The inner border is pieced from a medium square patch shape (Template KK), and the outer border is pieced using the small square patch shape again (Template JJ).

CUTTING OUT

Large Square: Cut 1 x 9½in (24.25cm) wide strip across the width of the fabric. From this cut 9½in x 9½in (24.25cm x 24.25cm) squares. Cut 2 in GP31CR, GP37MO, LC02TO, LC04BK, LC05TO, MN01DK, MN05DK, MN05RD, 1 in LC01BK and LC02BK. Reserve remaining strips and use for following templates.

Template JJ: Cut 3½in (9cm) wide strips across the width of the fabric. Each strip will give you 12 patches per 45in (114cm) wide fabric. Cut 19 in GP34MG, 18 in GP31CR, LC02TO, 17 in MN03RD, 16 in MN03DK, 15 in LC02BK, LC04BK, 14 in GP30BK, MN05RD, 11 in GP37MO, MN01DK, 10 in GP34BL, LC01BK, LC05TO, 9 in LC03AZ, LC03PE, MN05DK, 8 in GP34BR and LC03GN.

Template KK: Cut 5in (12.75cm) wide strips across the width of the fabric. Each strip will give you 8 patches per 45in (114cm) wide fabric. Cut 26 in SIF03 and SIF06.

Binding: Cut 7 strips 2½in (6.5cm) wide x width of fabric in GP01JG.

Backing:
Cut 1 piece 44in x 66in (112cm x 168cm) and 1 piece 41in x 66in (104cm x 168cm) in backing fabric.

MAKING THE QUILT

Use a ¼in (6mm) seam allowance throughout and refer to the quilt assembly diagram for fabric arrangement. Start by piecing the nine-patch blocks, each nine-patch block has 4 of one and 5 of another fabric. Following block assembly diagrams a and b make a total of 17 blocks. Alternating the nine-patch blocks with large squares, piece into 7 rows of 5 blocks. Join the rows to form the quilt centre.

MAKING THE BORDERS

Take the template KK squares and piece into 2 borders of 10 squares for the quilt top and bottom and 2 borders of 16 squares for the quilt sides. Note: The stripe direction is important for this border. Join to the quilt centre in the order indicated in the quilt assembly diagram. Take the remaining template JJ squares and piece into 2 borders of 18 squares for the top and bottom of the quilt and 2 borders of 26 squares for the quilt sides. Join to the quilt centre as before.

FINISHING THE QUILT

Press the quilt top. Seam the backing pieces using a ¼in (6mm) seam allowance to form a piece approx. 66in x 84in (168cm x 213.5cm). Layer the quilt top, batting and backing and baste together (see page 120). Using a dark red machine quilting tread quilt in a loose meandering pattern across the surface of the quilt. Trim the quilt edges and attach the binding (see page 121).

Quilt Assembly

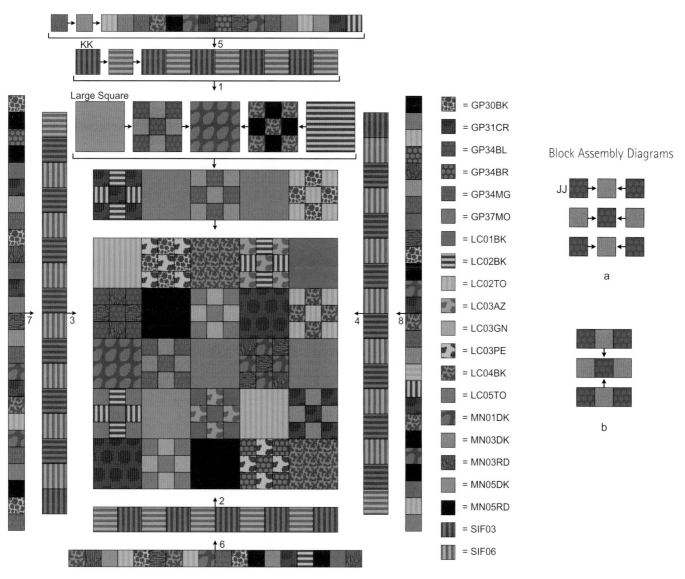

= GP30BK
= GP31CR
= GP34BL
= GP34BR
= GP34MG
= GP37MO
= LC01BK
= LC02BK
= LC02TO
= LC03AZ
= LC03GN
= LC03PE
= LC04BK
= LC05TO
= MN01DK
= MN03DK
= MN03RD
= MN05DK
= MN05RD
= SIF03
= SIF06

Block Assembly Diagrams

Mossy Radiation Quilt ★★★

KAFFE FASSETT

Once again I've borrowed a layout from an old British quilt, with this green bias, I think it has a more contemporary feel.

SIZE OF QUILT
The finished quilt will measure approx. 83¼ in x 83¼ in (211.5cm x 211.5cm).

MATERIALS
The quantities given are generous to allow for choice in fabric placement in the pieced triangle sections, see below for details.

Patchwork Fabrics:

BATIK CONFETTI
Moss   BKC03: ⅝yd (60cm)
DOUBLE IKAT CHECKERBOARD
Indigo   DIC03: ¼yd (25cm)
ROMAN GLASS
Leafy   GP01L: ⅜yd (35cm)
WILD ROSE
Lavender   GP26LV: ⅛yd (15cm)
Ochre   GP26OC: ¼yd (25cm)
LOTUS LEAF
Antique   GP29AN: ¾yd (70cm)

LEAVES
Black   GP30BK: 1 yd (90cm)
                            includes binding
Jade   GP30JA: ⅝yd (60cm)
Ochre   GP30OC: ¼yd (25cm)
ZINNIA
Antique   GP31AN: ¾yd (70cm)
PAISLEY STRIPE
Antique   GP32AN: ¼yd (25cm)
KIMONO
Cobalt/Turquoise GP33CT: ⅜yd (35cm)
Rust/Purple   GP33RP: 1¾yds (1.6m)
SPOOLS
Jade   GP34JA: ½yd (45cm)
BEACHBALLS
Jungle   GP37JG: ⅜yd (35cm)
SINGLE IKAT FEATHERS
Turquoise   SIF04: ⅛yd (15cm)
SINGLE IKAT WASH
Green   SIW04: ⅜yd (35cm)

SHOT COTTON
Jade   SC41: ⅜yd (35cm)

Backing Fabric: 5¼yds (4.8m)
We suggest these fabrics for backing:
KIMONO Cobalt/Turquoise GP33CT or Rust/Purple GP33RP
LOTUS LEAF Antique GP29AN

Binding:
LEAVES
Black   GP30BK: see patchwork fabrics

Batting:
90in x 90in (229cm x 229cm).

Quilting thread:
Toning machine quilting thread.

Templates:
see page 105.

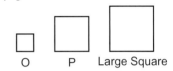

O   P   Large Square

PATCH SHAPES
The quilt is formed by a large central block surrounded by 8 borders - 5 simple borders (2 with corner posts) and 3 sections of pieced triangles. The central square block is a 4-patch block pieced from a large square cut to size. This is surrounded by simple border 1. The next section is the 1st pieced triangle section. The pieced triangle sections are made by stitching cut strips into a row, the triangles are then cut from the resulting row. This is surrounded by simple border 2. Next is the 2nd pieced triangle section, which is followed by border 3 which has corner posts (Template O). The 3rd pieced triangle section is then added followed by simple border 4 and simple border 5 which has corner posts (Template P).

CUTTING OUT
Large Square: Cut 8in (20.5cm) wide strips across the width of the fabric. Cut 2 in DIC03, and GP33RP. Reserve leftover strip and trim for template P.
Template O: Cut 3in (7.75cm) wide strips across the width of the fabric. Cut 4 in GP34JA.

Quilt Assembly

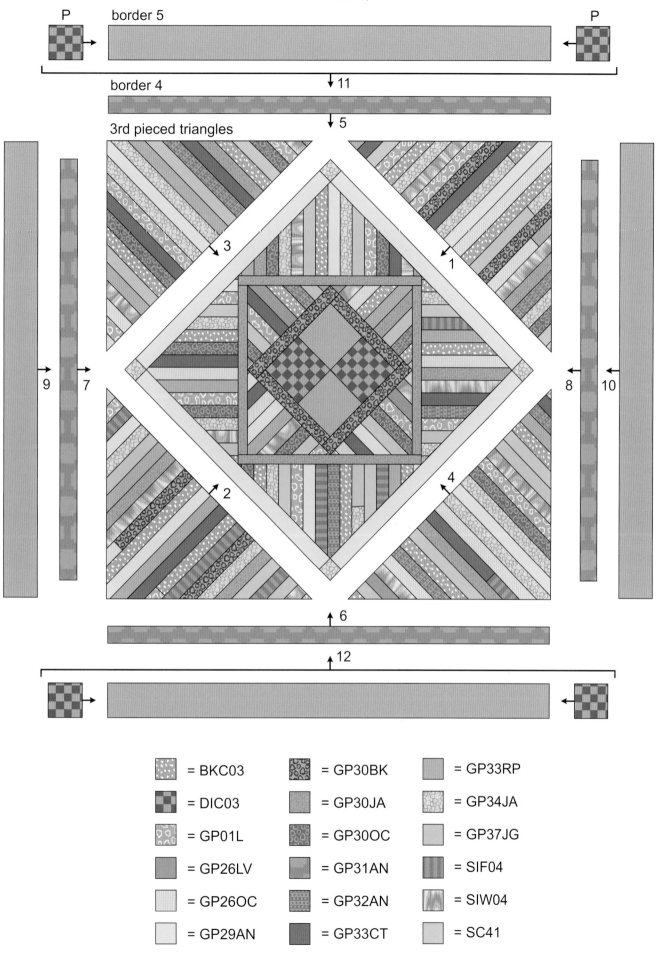

= BKC03	= GP30BK	= GP33RP
= DIC03	= GP30JA	= GP34JA
= GP01L	= GP30OC	= GP37JG
= GP26LV	= GP31AN	= SIF04
= GP26OC	= GP32AN	= SIW04
= GP29AN	= GP33CT	= SC41

1st pieced triangles

a

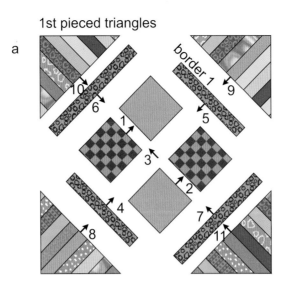

Start cutting 1in (2.5cm)
from the strip end
↓

1st Pieced Triangles

b

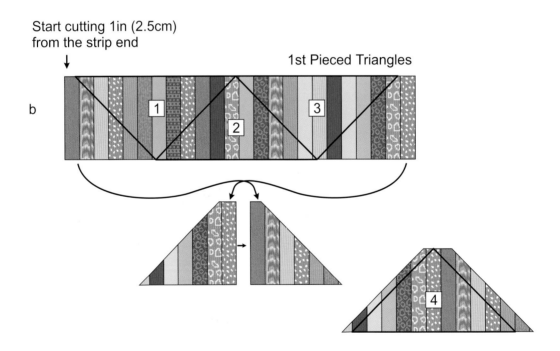

Template P: Cut 6in (15.25cm) wide strips across the width of the fabric. Cut 4 in DIC03.
Border 1: Cut 2 strips 2¹/₂in x 15¹/₂in (6.5cm x 39.5cm) and 2 strips 2¹/₂in x 19¹/₂in (6.5cm x 49.5cm) in GP30BK.
Border 2: Cut 2 strips 2in x 27³/₈in (5cm x 69.5cm) and 2 strips 2in x 30³/₈in (5cm x 77.25cm) in GP30JA.
Border 3: Cut 4 strips 3in x 42³/₄in (7.75cm x 108.5cm) in GP29AN.
Border 4: Cut 7 strips 3¹/₄in (8.25cm) x

the width of the fabric, join as necessary and cut 2 strips 3¹/₄in x 67¹/₄in (8.25cm x 171cm) and 2 strips 3¹/₄in x 72³/₄in (8.25cm x 184.75cm) in GP31AN.
Border 5: Cut 8 strips 6in (15.25cm) x the width of the fabric, join as necessary and cut 4 strips 6in x 74³/₄in (15.25cm x 190cm) in GP33RP.
Pieced Triangles: All other fabrics are cut into 2¹/₂in (6.5cm) strips and pieced to form rows.
1st Pieced triangles: Cut a total of 26

strips 2¹/₂in x 10³/₄in (6.5cm x 27.25cm).
2nd Pieced triangles: Cut a total of 36 strips 2¹/₂in x 16¹/₂in (6.5cm x 42cm).
3rd Pieced triangles: Cut a total of 52 strips 2¹/₂in x 25in (6.5cm x 63.5cm). Strips can be joined to prevent waste.

Binding: Cut 8 strips 2¹/₂in (6.5cm) wide x width of fabric in GP30BK.

Backing: Cut 2 pieces 45in x 90in (115cm x 229cm) in backing fabric.

MAKING THE QUILT

Use a 1/4in (6mm) seam allowance throughout and refer to the quilt assembly diagram for fabric placement. Piece the 4-patch centre block as shown in diagram a, add simple border 1 in the order indicated. Next piece the strips for the 1st triangle section into a row as shown in diagram b. Start cutting 1in (2.5cm) in from the end of the strip, cut 3 triangles (1, 2 & 3), then join the leftover section as shown in the diagram and cut the final triangle (4). The triangles will be slightly oversized. Join them to the quilt centre in the order shown in diagram a.

Trim to a generous 1/4in (6mm) OUTSIDE the corners of border 1.
Join border 2 to the quilt centre as shown in diagram c. Piece and cut the strips for the 2nd triangle section in the same way as the 1st triangle section. Join the sections to the quilt centre and trim to a generous 1/4in (6mm) OUTSIDE the corners of border 2.
Join border 3 to the quilt centre as shown in diagram c. Piece and cut the strips for the 3rd triangle section as before. Join to the quilt centre and trim to a generous 1/4in (6mm) OUTSIDE the corners of border 3.

Finally join borders 4 and 5 in the order shown in the quilt assembly diagram.

FINISHING THE QUILT

Press the quilt top. Seam the backing pieces using a 1/4in (6mm) seam allowance to form a piece approx. 90in x 90in (229cm x 229cm). Layer the quilt top, batting and backing and baste together (see page 120). Using a toning machine quilting thread, quilt-in-the-ditch around the centre 4-patch squares and all the simple borders. Quilt along alternate seams in the pieced triangles sections. Trim the quilt edges and attach the binding (see page 121).

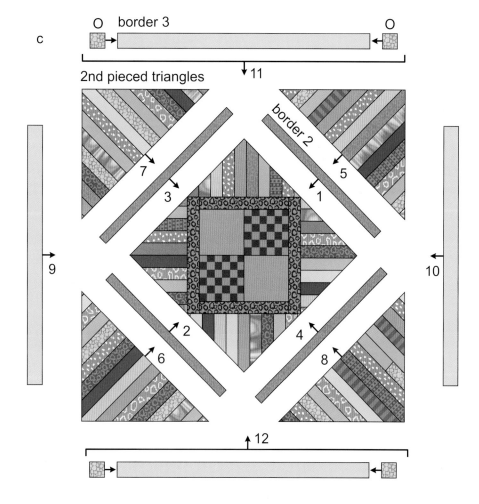

Two Birds in a Sunny Garden Panel ★

JANET BOLTON

This is the beginning. The panel, complete in itself, is open to interpretation. Use it as a starting point making changes by moving the different pieces around.

SIZE OF PANEL
The finished panel will measure approx. 20in x 12in (51cm x 30.5cm).

MATERIALS
Patchwork Fabrics:
SHOT COTTON
Slate	SC04:	1/8yd (15cm)
Opal	SC05:	1/8yd (15cm)
Bittersweet	SC10:	1/8yd (15cm)
Sage	SC17:	1/8yd (15cm)
Duck Egg	SC26:	1/8yd (15cm)
Blush	SC28:	3/8yd (35cm)
Mushroom	SC31:	1/8yd (15cm)
Watermelon	SC33:	1/8yd (15cm)
Mist	SC48:	1/8yd (15cm)
Shell	SC49:	1/4yd (25cm)
Forget-Me-Not	SC51:	1/8yd (15cm)

Appliqué Fabrics:
Small quantities of the following fabrics:
BATIK CONFETTI
Tomato	BKC01
KASHMIR	
Black	GP25BK
SHOT COTTON	
Mustard	SC16

Sage	SC17
Smoky	SC20
Duck Egg	SC26
Mushroom	SC31
Cobalt	SC45

Backing Fabric:
SHOT COTTON
Smoky	SC20: 1/2yd (45cm)

Thread:
Standard cotton sewing thread in maroon and natural, used double.
Neutral hand quilting thread.

Buttons:
A selection of mother-of-pearl and shell buttons from the Rowan collection.

Templates:
see page 112.

PATCH SHAPES
This panel is constructed from a selection of rectangles and strips cut to size.
Instead of batting a layer of shot cotton is used for the interlining. Another layer

is used for the backing. Although we have provided basic appliqué shapes you can cut your own, tucking and pulling them into shape. Don't be too concerned with getting the shapes exactly right.

CUTTING OUT
Piece 1: Cut 1 rectangle 91/2in x 5in (24.25cm x 12.75cm) in SC49
Piece 2: Cut 1 rectangle 91/2in x 51/2in (24.25cm x 14cm) in SC28
Piece 3: Cut 1 rectangle 51/2in x 5in (14cm x 12.75cm) in SC28
Piece 4: Cut 1 rectangle 3in x 5in (7.5cm x 12.75cm) in SC49
Piece 5: Cut 1 rectangle 2in x 5in (6cm x 12.75cm) in SC28
Piece 6: Cut 1 rectangle 8in x 51/2in (20.25cm x 14cm) in SC28
Piece 7: Cut 1 rectangle 2in x 51/2in (5cm x 14cm) in SC28
Piece 8: Cut 1 strip 1in x 91/2in (2.5cm x 24.25cm) in SC10
Piece 9: Cut 1 strip 1in x 7in (2.5cm x 17.75cm) in SC26
Piece 10: Cut 1 strip 1in x 3in (2.5cm x 7.75cm) in SC33

Piece 11: Cut 1 strip 1in x 5¹/₄in (2.5cm x 13.5cm) in SC17

Piece 12: Cut 1 strip 1in x 5³/₄in (2.5cm x 14.5cm) in SC48

Piece 13: Cut 1 strip 1¹/₄in x 6¹/₂in (3.25cm x 16.5cm) in SC33

Piece 14: Cut 1 strip 1¹/₄in x 4¹/₂in (3.25cm x 11.5cm) in SC51

Piece 15: Cut 1 strip 1¹/₄in x 3³/₄in (3.25cm x 9.5cm) in SC17

Piece 16: Cut 1 square 1¹/₄in x 1¹/₄in (3.25cm x 3.25cm) in SC33

Piece 17: Cut 1 strip 1¹/₄in x 6¹/₂in (3.25cm x 16.5cm) in SC31

Piece 18: Cut 1 strip 1¹/₂in x 16¹/₂in (3.75cm x 42cm) in SC48

Piece 19: Cut 1 strip 1¹/₂in x 13in (3.75cm x 33cm) in SC05

Piece 20: Cut 1 strip 1¹/₂in x 13in (3.75cm x 33cm) in SC33

Piece 21: Cut 1 strip 1¹/₂in x 16¹/₂in (3.75cm x 42cm) in SC04

Interlining: Cut 1 rectangle 20in x 12in (51cm x 30.5cm) in SC28

Backing: Cut 1 rectangle 21in x 13in (53.25cm x 33cm) in SC20

MAKING THE BACKGROUND

Use a ¹/₄in (6mm) seam allowance throughout. Lay out the first set of cut shapes as shown in diagram a. Join the shapes as shown. Take the next set of cut shapes and lay out as shown in diagram b. Join the shapes as shown except for the top and bottom borders. Press a ¹/₄in (6mm) seam allowance along the side borders and then join the top and bottom borders as shown. These will be longer than the panel at this stage. Press ¹/₄in (6mm) seam allowance along the extended edges of the top and bottom

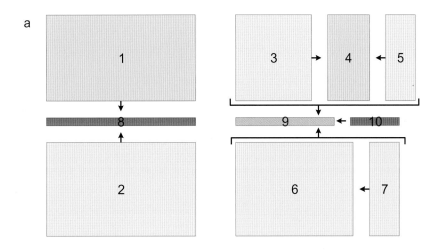

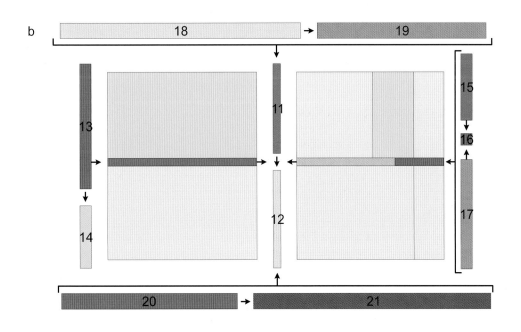

borders and along the outside edges of the borders. Fold the extended border ends in and pin into place.

Layer the background with the interlining and backing. Finger-turn the backing in so that a small amount shows from the front of the panel. Let the amount that shows vary for a lively feeling. Pin and stitch the layers together using a small stabbing stitch around the outside edges, changing the thread colour to enhance the visual design.

APPLIQUÉ
Pin the appliqué shapes to the background and when you are happy with the placement stitch to the background by hand, see the Hand Appliqué section in Patchwork Know How on page 119. We have provided shapes for the birds, wings and 2 sizes of leaf shapes, the shapes include a ¼in (6mm) seam allowance. The bird's legs finish to about ¼in x 1½in (6mm x 3.75cm), plant stems finish to about ¼in – ⅜in (6mm – 9mm) wide. The squares vary in size from ⅝in – ¾in (1.5cm – 2cm) square. The flowers are selectively cut from GP25BK. Sew the buttons in place.

QUILTING
Using neutral quilting thread hand quilt over the background areas only as shown in the photograph on page 45.

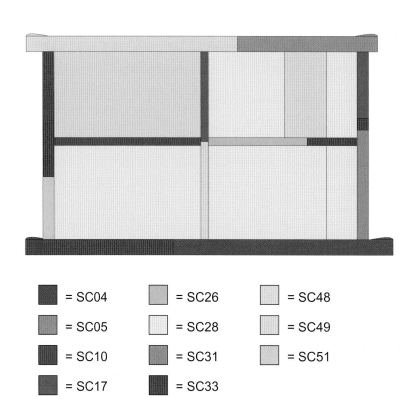

■ = SC04		■ = SC26		■ = SC48	
■ = SC05		■ = SC28		■ = SC49	
■ = SC10		■ = SC31		■ = SC51	
■ = SC17		■ = SC33			

Kaleidoscope Cushion ★

Betsy Mennesson

SIZE OF CUSHION
The finished cushion will measure approx. 24in x 24in (61cm x 61cm).

MATERIALS
Patchwork Fabrics:
LOTUS LEAF
Antique   GP29AN: 5/8 yd (60cm)
SINGLE IKAT WASH
Green   SIW06: 1/2yd (45cm)

Cushion Reverse:
SHOT COTTON
Grape   SC47: 3/4yd (70cm)

Binding for Cushion Reverse:
LOTUS LEAF
Antique   GP29AN:
                 see patchwork fabrics

Lining Fabric:
Muslin or calico
1 piece 24 1/2in x 24 1/2in (62.5cm x 62.5cm).
2 pieces 24 1/2in x 15 1/2in (62.5cm x 39.25cm).

Batting:
1 piece 24 1/2in x 24 1/2in (62.5cm x 62.5cm).
2 pieces 24 1/2in x 15 1/2in (62.5cm x 39.25cm).

Quilting thread:
Toning machine quilting thread.

Templates:
see page 106.

W   X

PATCH SHAPES
The cushion front is made from two triangles shapes. The large triangles (Template W) are pieced into an octagon. A second triangle shape (Template X) is used to make the blocks square. Four blocks form the cushion front. The reverse is made in an envelope style.

CUTTING OUT
Template W: Cut 6 7/8in- (17.5cm-) wide strips across the width of the fabric. Each strip will give you 13 patches per 45in (114cm) wide fabric. Cut 16 in GP29AN and SIW04. Reserve the remaining strip for template X.
Template X: Trim the reserved strip to 4 3/8in (11.25cm). Cut 12 in GP29AN and 4 in SIW04.

Cushion Reverse: Cut 2 pieces 24 1/2in x 15 1/2in (62.5cm x 39.25cm) in SC47.

Binding for Cushion Reverse: Cut 2 strips 2 1/2in x 24 1/2in (6.5cm x 62.5cm) in GP29AN.

MAKING THE CUSHION FRONT
Use a 1/4in (6mm) seam allowance throughout and refer to the cushion assembly diagram for fabric placement. Make 4 blocks following diagrams a, b, c and d. Join the blocks as shown in the cushion assembly diagram. Press the cushion front, layer with the batting and lining and baste together, either quilt freely as Betsy has done as shown in the photograph, or for a simpler look quilt in the ditch.

MAKING THE CUSHION REVERSE
Layer each of the cushion reverse pieces with batting and lining and baste together. Meander quilt across the surface. Bind one long edge of each piece with the strips in GP29AN.

FINISHING THE CUSHION
Place the cushion front right sides together with the two back pieces, overlapping the bound edges of the backs in the centre to form an envelope effect. Stitch the cushion front to the backs all around the edge. Trim back any excess batting in the seam to reduce bulk, turn the cushion through and insert pad through the envelope style back.

= GP29AN

= SIW04

Rowan's Baby Blocks Quilt ★ ★

KEIKO GOKE

Keiko has used bright prints and shot cottons in this colourful 'scrap' quilt.

SIZE OF QUILT
The finished quilt will measure approx. 39½in x 44½in (100.5cm x 113cm).

MATERIALS
Note: We have drawn and specified the fabrics accurately for Keiko's quilt, however it is designed as a scrap quilt and you could use leftovers from other Rowan projects. Also the Swiggle and Organic stripe fabrics are 'good value' as each has 4 very different design elements to separate and use.

Patchwork Fabrics:
ROMAN GLASS
Gold	GP01G: ⅛yd (15cm)
Red	GP01R: ⅛yd (15cm)

PAPERWEIGHT
Lime	GP20LM: ⅛yd (15cm)
Sludge	GP20SL: ⅛yd (15cm)

ORGANIC STRIPE
Blue	GP21BL: ¼yd (25cm)
Green	GP21GN: ⅛yd (15cm)
Lime	GP21LM: ⅛yd (15cm)
Pink	GP21PK: ¼yd (25cm)

SWIGGLE STRIPE
Antique	GP22AN: ¼yd (25cm)
Blue	GP22BL: ¼yd (25cm)
Ochre	GP22OC: ⅛yd (15cm)
Pink	GP22PK: ¼yd (25cm)

DIAGONAL POPPY
Blue	GP24BL: ⅛yd (15cm)
Lavender	GP24LV: ¼yd (25cm)

KASHMIR
Blue	GP25BL: ⅛yd (15cm)
Raspberry	GP25RS: ⅛yd (15cm)

LOTUS LEAF
Blue	GP29BL: ¼yd (25cm)
Red	GP29RD: ¼yd (25cm)

LEAVES
Blue	GP30BL: ⅛yd (15cm)
Red	GP30RD: ⅛yd (15cm)

ZINNIA
Blue	GP31BL: ⅛yd (15cm)
Crimson	GP31CR: ¼yd (25cm)
Lime	GP31LM: ¼yd (25cm)

PAISLEY STRIPE
Blue	GP32BL: ⅛yd (15cm)
Pastel	GP32PT: ¼yd (25cm)
Red	GP32RD: ¼yd (25cm)

KIMONO
Crimson/Magenta	GP33CM: ¼yd (25cm)
Cobalt/Turquoise	GP33CT: ⅛yd (15cm)

SHOT COTTON
Persimmon	SC07: ⅛yd (15cm)
Tangerine	SC11: ⅛yd (15cm)
Lavender	SC14: ¼yd (25cm)
Grass	SC27: ⅛yd (15cm)
Watermelon	SC33: ⅛yd (15cm)
Lemon	SC34: ¼yd (25cm)
Sunshine	SC35: ⅛yd (15cm)
Jade	SC41: ¼yd (25cm)
Lime	SC43: ⅛yd (15cm)
Scarlet	SC44: ⅜yd (35cm) includes inner border.
Forget-Me-Not	SC51: ¼yd (25cm)

BROAD STRIPE
	BS23: ⅛yd (15cm)

Inner Border
SHOT COTTON
Scarlet	SC44: see patchwork fabrics

Outer Border
ZINNIA
Magenta	GP31MG: ⅝yd (60cm)

Outer Border corner posts are included in patchwork fabrics.

Backing Fabric
Note: The backing for this quilt was pieced from the fabrics listed below, alternatively use leftover strips to piece a backing.
ORGANIC STRIPE
Brown	GP21BR: ⅜yd (35cm)

LOTUS LEAF
Ochre	GP29OC: ⅝yd (60cm)
Pastel	GP29PT: ⅝yd (60cm)

Binding:
SHOT COTTON
Persimmon	SC07: ⅜yd (35cm)

Batting:
45in x 50in (115cm x 127cm).

Block Assembly

a

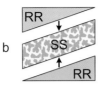

b

c

Row Assembly Diagram

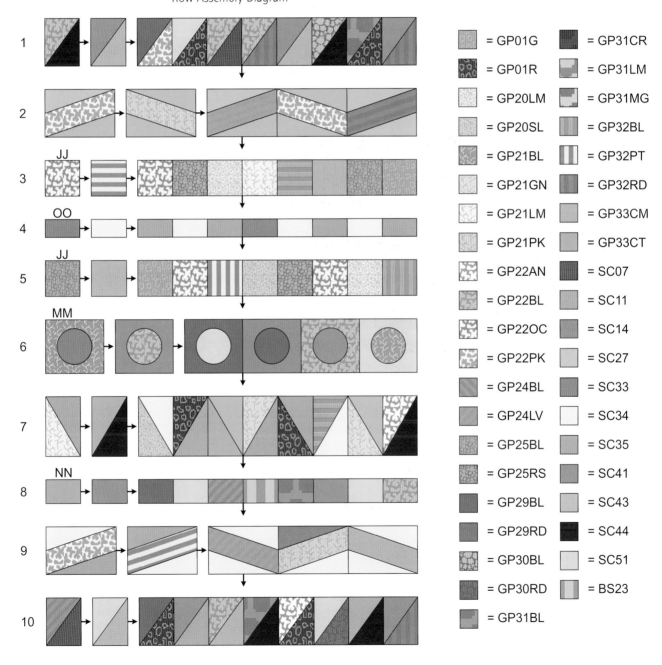

= GP01G	= GP31CR
= GP01R	= GP31LM
= GP20LM	= GP31MG
= GP20SL	= GP32BL
= GP21BL	= GP32PT
= GP21GN	= GP32RD
= GP21LM	= GP33CM
= GP21PK	= GP33CT
= GP22AN	= SC07
= GP22BL	= SC11
= GP22OC	= SC14
= GP22PK	= SC27
= GP24BL	= SC33
= GP24LV	= SC34
= GP25BL	= SC35
= GP25RS	= SC41
= GP29BL	= SC43
= GP29RD	= SC44
= GP30BL	= SC51
= GP30RD	= BS23
= GP31BL	

Quilting thread:
Multi-coloured embroidery thread.

Templates:
see page 109, 110, 111.

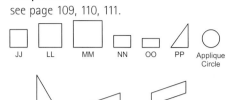

PATCH SHAPES
The quilt centre is made up in rows.
Row 1: Uses 1 triangle patch shape (Template PP) pieced into blocks and then into a row.
Row 2: Uses 1 triangle patch shape (Template RR) and 1 lozenge patch shape (Template SS) pieced into blocks and then into a row. Some of the patch shapes are reversed.
Row 3: Uses 1 square patch shape (Template JJ) pieced into a row.
Row 4: Uses 1 rectangle patch shape (Template OO) pieced into a row.
Row 5: As row 3.
Row 6: Uses 1 rectangle patch shape (Template MM) pieced into a row, each rectangle has a hand appliquéd circle

(Appliqué Circle).
Row 7: Uses 1 triangle patch shape (Template QQ) pieced into blocks and then into a row. Some of the patch shapes are reversed.
Row 8: Uses 1 rectangle patch shape (Template NN) pieced into a row.
Row 9: As row 2.
Row 10: As row 1.
The rows are joined to form the quilt centre and then surrounded by a narrow inner border. A wide outer border with corner posts (Template LL) is then added to finish the quilt.

CUTTING OUT
To reduce waste we suggest drawing round the templates for each patch shape onto the fabric for the best fit before cutting. This will allow the best use of Organic and Swiggle stripe fabrics which have 4 design elements per fabric. Refer to the photographs for design element placement. You can also vary the stripe direction by rotating the templates for striped fabrics,
Template JJ: Cut 4 in GP22OC, 2 in GP01G, GP20LM, GP25BL, GP25RS, GP32BL, GP32PT, GP33CM, 1 in GP20SL and GP21LM

Template MM: Cut 1 in GP21BL, GP22BL, GP29BL, SC14, SC41 and SC51.
Template NN: Cut 2 in SC41, SC51, 1 in GP22BL, GP24BL, GP29BL, GP31BL, GP33CT and BS23.
Template OO: Cut 4 in SC34, SC35 and 2 in SC33.
Template PP: Cut 5 in SC41, 4 in GP01R, GP22BL, GP33CM, SC44, 3 in GP32RD, SC51, 2 in GP29BL, GP31BL, SC07, 1 in GP22AN, GP22PK, GP24BL, GP30BL, GP30RD, GP33CT and SC11.
Template QQ and reverse QQ: Cut 2 in SC43, 1 in GP01R, GP20SL, GP21GN, GP21LM, GP33CM, SC11, SC34 and SC35. Reverse the template by turning it over, cut 2 in SC44, 1 in GP01R, GP21GN, GP22AN, GP32BL, GP33CM, SC11, SC34 and SC35.
Template RR and reverse RR: Cut 4 in SC27, 3 in SC34, 2 in SC43, 1 in SC11, SC33 and SC35. Reverse the template by turning it over, cut 4 in SC34 and SC43.
Template SS and Reverse SS: Cut 2 in GP22PK, 1 in GP21PK, GP24LV, GP32PT, GP32RD. Reverse the template by turning it over, cut 1 in GP21PK, GP22PK, GP24LV and GP33CM.
Appliqué Circle: Cut 1 in GP21BL, GP22BL, GP29BL, SC33, SC41 and SC51.

Quilt Assembly Diagram

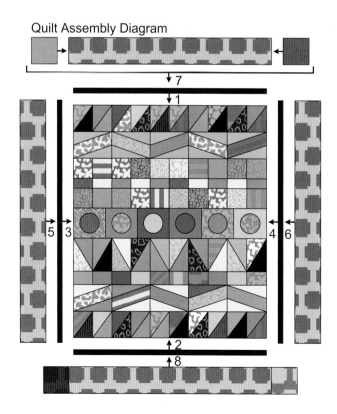

Inner Border: Cut 4 strips 1¼in (3.25cm) x the width of the fabric. From these cut 2 strips 1¼in x 37in (3.25cm x 94cm) and 2 strips 1¼in x 30½in (3.25cm x 77.5cm) in SC44.

Outer Border: Cut 4 strips 4½in (11.5cm) x the width of the fabric. From these cut 2 strips 4½in x 37in (11.5cm x 94cm) and 2 strips 4½in x 32in (11.5cm x 81.25cm) in GP31AN.

Template LL: (Outer border corners) Cut 1 in GP29RD, GP31CR, GP31LM & GP33CM.

Binding: Cut 4 strips 2½in (6.5cm) wide x width of fabric in SC07.

Backing: Cut 2 pieces 45in x 19½in (115cm x 49.5cm) 1 in GP29OC and 1 in GP29PT. Cut 1 piece 45in x 12½in (115cm x 31.75cm) in GP21BR. Alternatively piece a backing measuring 45in x 50in (115cm x 127cm) from leftover strips.

MAKING THE ROWS
Use a ¼in (6mm) seam allowance throughout. Refer to the row assembly diagram for fabric placement. The rows are numbered 1-10. Piece the blocks for Rows 1 and 10 following block assembly diagram a. Piece the blocks for Rows 2 and 9 following block assembly diagram b. Piece the blocks for Row 7 following block assembly diagram c. Hand appliqué a circle onto each template MM rectangle for row 6, see the Hand Appliqué section in Patchwork Know How on page 119 for instructions. Piece all the remaining rows.

MAKING THE QUILT
Join the rows to form the quilt centre.

Add the inner border in the order indicated in the quilt assembly diagram. Add the side borders, join a corner post to each end of the top and bottom borders, and add to the quilt centre.

FINISHING THE QUILT
Press the quilt top. Seam the backing pieces using a ¼in (6mm) seam allowance to form a piece approx. 45in x 50in (115cm x 127cm) with the Organic stripe fabric separating the 2 colourways of Lotus Leaf fabric (or use your backing pieced from leftover strips). Layer the quilt top, batting and backing and baste together (see page 120). Hand quilt using multi-coloured embroidery threads as shown in the quilting diagram. Trim the quilt edges and attach the binding (see page 121).

Quilting Diagram

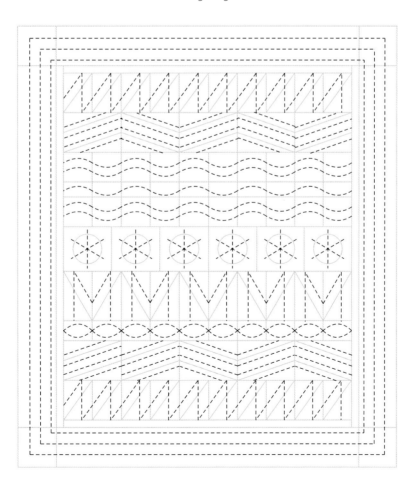

Patchwork Cats ★★

KEIKO GOKE

Keiko's patchwork cats are sure to appeal to little people and are fun to make! They are also a good way to use up scraps from other projects such as the Rowan's Baby Blocks Quilt.

SIZE OF CATS
Large: Approx. 15in (38cm).
Small: Approx. 12in (30.5cm).

MATERIALS
Patchwork Fabrics:
Assorted scraps totalling 1/2yd (45cm) per cat.

You will also need:
Toy stuffing.
Dark embroidery thread.
Clear template plastic.

Templates:
The templates for these cats are printed at 50% of true size. Photocopy at 200% before using. See page 114.

MAKING THE CATS
First make templates using clear template plastic for the cat shape and tail shape.

The shapes include a 1/4in (6mm) seam allowance. Make up a piece of patchwork approx. 17in x 12in (43cm x 30.5cm) for the large cat and 15in x 10in (38cm x 25.5cm) for the small cat as shown in diagram a. You could use triangles, squares or random strips. Position a larger fabric patch for the cat's face.

With the patchwork right side up mark the cutting line by drawing around the template, but don't cut yet! Mark a face on the right side of the patchwork and embroider, using the photograph as a guide. Make a second piece of patchwork or use a single fabric for the cat's back, pin the front and back fabrics **wrong** sides together and cut both fabrics on the drawn line.

Cut 2 rectangles of fabric for the tail, 9in x 6in (23cm x 15.5cm) for the large cat

and 7 1/2in x 4 1/2in (19cm x 11.5cm) for the small cat. Place the rectangles right sides together and cut out the tail shapes. Run 2 lines of stitching around the tail leaving the straight cut end open for stuffing as shown in diagram b. Stuff firmly leaving the last 3/4in (2cm) free.

Separate the cat front and back and match carefully with **right** sides together, position the tail between the front and back so that the stuffed section is up against the sewing line. Sew around the cat with 2 lines of stitching for extra strength, using a zipper foot on your machine will help when stitching the tail in place. Leave a gap as shown in diagram c for stuffing. Clip the seam allowance around the ears, turn the cat through and stuff firmly. Slip stitch the gap closed and catch stitch the tail at the top to form a 'handle'.

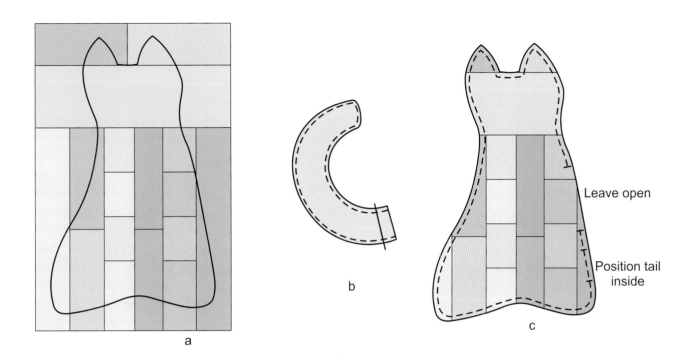

a

b

Leave open

Position tail inside

c

Postcard Quilt ★★★★

LIZA PRIOR LUCY

People often ask how we come up with the names for our quilts. While Kaffe and I were finishing up the quilts for the V & A Museum book, we visited with Pauline. She pulled out a pile of postcards that she had saved over the years and showed us a V & A quilt image that we had never seen. We jotted down the coded number for the quilt and the three of us went down to London and asked the museum to show us the quilt. We were stunned by what we saw. Immediately Kaffe and I began to work on the quilt to try and get it done for our big book but it just couldn't be accomplished in the short time we had left. The quilt was so wonderful that I plugged ahead and finished it anyway and so here it is, the 'Postcard' Quilt.

The original quilt was done in reds, greens and ecrus. It has faded over the years and now looks more like corals, sages and toast colours. This blue version is entirely different in feel from the original and yet maintains the wonderful structure. When I completed the blue version I had just been sent yardage of Carla Miller's new fabric collection. Some of the colours were so like the faded ones in the original. They also looked like the kinds of textures and colours one would see on an elaborate tile floor. I had to make this second version to be included here. It's not quite done, but I just had to show you! (See photograph on page 9).

This quilt is quite a piecing challenge and a lot of fun to do. Because of the various angles and piecing difficulties some of the borders are best made too long and then just chopped off to fit. This is certainly in keeping with the way the original quilt was made, back in the days before rotary cutters, acrylic rulers and computers. Many thanks to Andrea at Electric Quilt for helping me get the templates and working diagrams just right.

SIZE OF QUILT
The finished quilt will measure approx. 84in x 84in (213.5cm x 213.5cm).

MATERIALS
Patchwork Fabrics:
Roman Glass
Red   GP01R: 1/4yd (25cm)
PEONY
Blue   GP17BL: 1 1/4yds (1.15m)
Violet   GP17VI: 1/2yd (45cm)
PAPERWEIGHT
Cobalt   GP20CB: 5/8yd (60cm)
Pastel   GP20PT: 1/4yd (25cm)
Sludge   GP20SL: 1 3/8yds (1.3m)
ORGANIC STRIPE
Blue   GP21BL: 5/8yd (60cm)
PANSY
Blue   GP23BL: 3/8yd (35cm)
DIAGONAL POPPY
Blue   GP24BL: 1/4yd (25cm)
Duck Egg   GP24DE: 1/8yd (15cm)
KASHMIR
Aqua   GP25AQ: 1/2yd (45cm)
Blue   GP25BL: 1/4yd (25cm)
Raspberry   GP25RS: 3/8yd (35cm)
WILD ROSE
Pastel   GP26PT: 1/4yd (25cm)
LOTUS LEAF
Pastel   GP29PT: 1 yd (90cm)
LEAVES
Blue   GP30BL: 3/8yd (35cm)
PAISLEY STRIPE
Blue   GP32BL: 1 yd (90cm)
Misty   GP32MS: 3/4yd (70cm)
KIMONO
Crimson/Magenta GP33CM: 1/4yd (25cm)
SPOOLS
Blue   GP34BL: 1 1/2yds (1.4m)
Lavender   GP34LV: 3/8yd (35cm)
DOTTED LEAVES
French Blue   LC03FB: 1/4yd (25cm)
SHOT COTTON
Raspberry   SC08: 1/2yd (45cm)
Apple   SC39: 3/8yd (35cm)
Jade   SC41: 1/8yd (15cm)
SINGLE IKAT WASH
Lavender   SIW05: 1/4yd (25cm)

Backing Fabric: 5 1/4yds (4.8m)
We suggest these fabrics for backing:
PAPERWEIGHT Sludge GP20SL
SPOOLS Blue GP34BL or Lavender GP34LV

Bias Binding:
PAISLEY STRIPE
Blue   GP32BL: 3/4yd (70cm)

Batting:
90in x 90in (229cm x 229cm).

Quilting thread:
Toning machine quilting thread.

Templates:
see pages 115-117

PATCH SHAPES
This quilt is a series of ten borders around a medallion centre. The cutting and piecing instructions are given for the centre and each border in order. **We suggest cutting and piecing as you go, however please read the whole instruction carefully and make sure you allow fabric for larger template shapes which come later in the process.** Borders 3 and 4 are made oversize and trimmed to fit (some steam and blocking may be needed to make these behave), all others are made to fit,

but because of bias, tiny pieces and odd shapes it will be necessary to occasionally ease one border to the next. It is NOT recommended that you trim each border or 'square up' each time you make a round. The fabric is flexible and forgiving. Many of the templates are odd sizes so careful cutting is very important, however we have not given templates for some of the simple square shapes, just the sizes you will need to cut.

CUTTING OUT AND PIECING
Centre
Template Centre A: Cut 1 in GP20PT.
Template Centre B: Cut 4 in GP30BL.
Template Centre C: Cut 4 in GP20PT and SC39. Total 8 patches.
Template Centre D: Cut 4 in GP24DE.
Template Centre E: Cut 12 in GP32MS, 8 in GP17BL and 4 in GP30BL. Total 24 patches.
Template Centre F: Cut 12 in GP20CB.
Template Centre G: Cut 32 in GP20PT

and 8 in GP20CB. Total 40 patches.

Piece the centre as shown in Diagram 1, following the stages as numbered.

Border 1: Plain with Corner Posts
Corner Posts: Cut 4 squares 1½in x 1½in (3.75cm) in SC39.
Borders: Cut 4 strips 12½in x 1½in (31.75cm x 3.75cm) in GP24BL.

Join 1 border to each side of the quilt, join a corner post to each end of the remaining 2 borders and add to the quilt, as shown in Diagram 1.

Border 2: Flying Geese
Template Border 2 A: Cut 56 in GP17VI.
Template Border 2 B: Cut 112 in SC08.
Template Border 2 C: Cut 4 in GP20PT and GP30BL. Total 8 patches.

Piece the template A and B patches into

Diagram 1

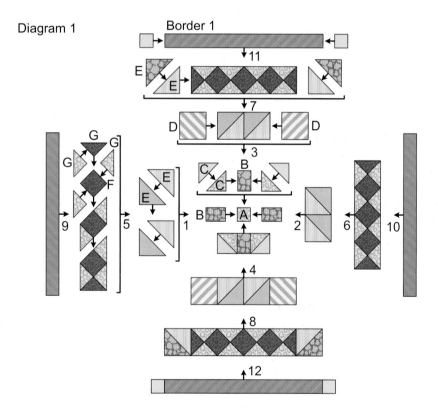

Diagram 2

blocks as shown in Diagram 2. Piece the blocks into 4 rows of 14 blocks. Join 1 row to each side of the quilt. Piece the template C patches into 4 squares, join 1 to each end of the remaining block rows. Add to the quilt as shown in Diagram 3.

Border 3: Card Trick
Template Border 3 A: Cut 28 in GP23BL and 16 in GP25RS.
Template Border 3 B: Cut 80 in SIW05.
Corner Posts: Cut 4 squares 3¹/₄in x 3¹/₄in (8.25cm x 8.25cm) in GP24DE.

Piece 4 borders as shown in Diagram 4. Trim each to 18¹/₂in (47cm). Join 1 border to each side of the quilt, join a corner post to each end of the remaining 2 borders and add to the quilt, as shown in Diagram 3.

Border 4: Diamonds
Template Border 4 A: Cut 32 in GP21BL, GP25AQ and GP32MS. Total 96 patches.
Template Border 4 B: Cut 64 in GP21BL.
Corner Posts: Cut a total of 16 squares 2¹/₂in x 2¹/₂in (6.5cm x 6.5cm), 8 in GP17VI and GP20CB.

Piece 4 borders as shown in Diagram 5. Trim each to 24in (61cm). Join 1 border to each side of the quilt. Piece the corner posts into 4 patch blocks as shown in Diagram 6 and join 1 to each end of the remaining borders, and add to the quilt, as shown in Diagram 3.

Border 5: 9-patch on Point
Template Border 5 A: Cut 26 in SC08, 24 in GP25AQ, 23 in GP17VI, GP32MS, 22 in GP25RS, GP26PT, 20 in GP25BL, 18 in GP30BL, 14 in GP20CB, 10 in GP23BL, SC41 and 4 in SC39. Total 216 patches.
Template Border 5 B: Cut 40 in GP20SL.
Template Border 5 C: Cut 16 in GP20SL.
Corner Posts: Cut 4 squares 5³/₄in x 5³/₄in (14.5cm x 14.5cm) in GP17BL.

Piece a total of 24 9-patch blocks as shown in Diagram 7. Piece into 4 borders of 6 blocks using the template B and C patches to fill in the edges and ends as shown in diagram 8. Add 1 border to each side of the quilt. Join a corner post to each end of the remaining 2 borders and add to the quilt, as shown in Diagram 8 (see opposite).

Border 6: Plain with Pieced Corner Posts
Template Border 6 A: Cut 4 in GP24BL and SC39. Total 8 Patches.

Diagram 3
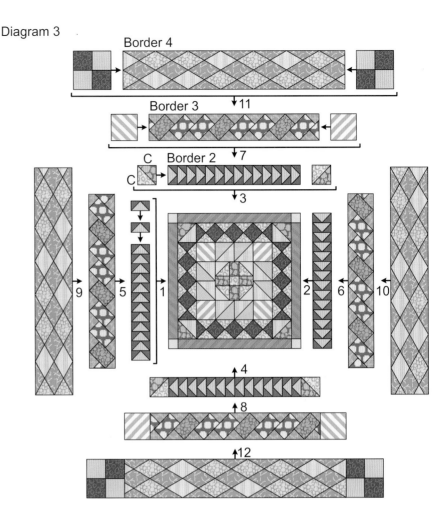

Diagram 4
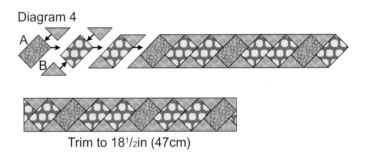
Trim to 18¹/₂in (47cm)

Diagram 5
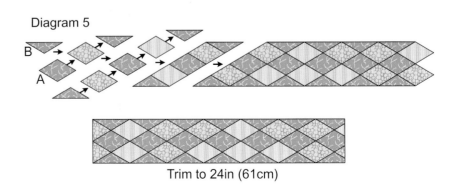
Trim to 24in (61cm)

Diagram 6

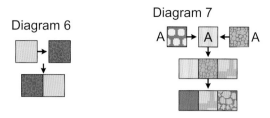

Diagram 7

A → A ← A

Diagram 8

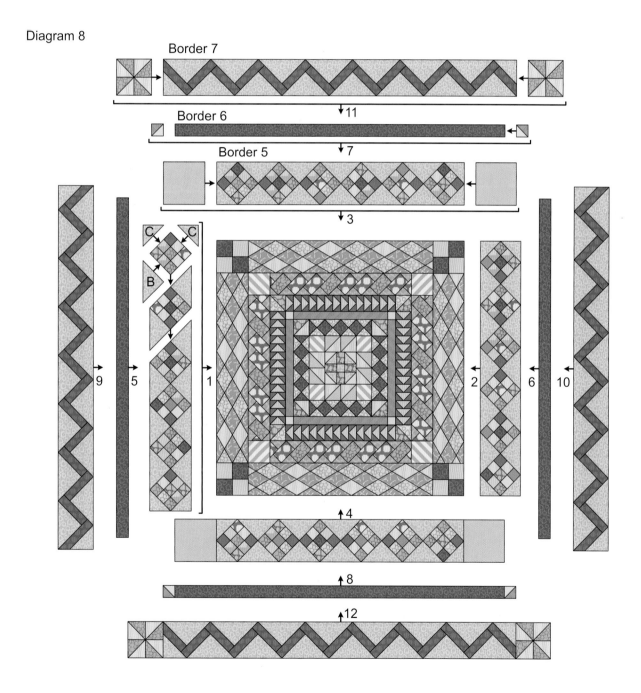

Border 7

↓11

Border 6

↓7

Border 5

↓3

9   5   1

2   6   10

↑4

↑8

↑12

Borders: Cut 4 strips 42¹/₂in x 2in (108cm x 5cm) in GP20CB.

Join 1 border to each side of the quilt. Piece the template A patches to make 4 squares, join 1 to each end of the remaining borders and add to the quilt, as shown in Diagram 8.

Border 7: Streak of Lightning
Template Border 7 A: Cut 52 in GP34BL.
Template Border 7 B: Cut 4 in GP34BL.
Template Border 7 C: Cut 4 in GP34BL.
Template Border 7 D: Cut 56 in GP20SL.
Template Border 7 E: Cut 8 in GP20SL.
Template Border 7 F: Cut 16 in GP25BL and GP32MS. Total 32 patches.

Piece 4 borders as shown in Diagram 9. Join 1 border to each side of the quilt. Piece 4 corner blocks as shown in diagram 10 and join 1 to each end of the remaining 2 borders and add to the quilt, as shown in Diagram 8.

Border 8: Flying Geese
Template Border 8 A: Cut 80 in GP29PT.
Template Border 8 B: Cut 160 in GP32BL.
Template Border 8 C: Cut 4 in GP34BL and GP34LV. Total 8 patches.
Template Border 8 D: Cut 16 in SC39.

Piece the template A and B patches into blocks as shown in Diagram 2.

Piece the blocks into 4 rows of 20 blocks. Join 1 row to each side of the quilt. Piece 4 corner posts using the template C and D patches as shown in Diagram 11 using the inset seam method (see Patchwork Know How on page 119), join 1 to each end of the remaining block rows. Add to the quilt as shown in Diagram 12.

Border 9: 9-patch on Point
Template Border 9 A: Cut 34 in GP29PT, 31 in GP01R, 28 in GP25RS, GP26PT, GP32MS, 27 in SC08, 26 in GP34LV, 22 in GP17VI, GP33CM, 13 in GP20CB, GP34BL, 10 in GP21BL, 9 in GP24BL, GP30BL, 7 in GP23BL, GP32BL, 6 in GP25AQ and 4 in GP25BL. Total 324 patches.
Template Border 9 B: Cut 64 in GP17BL.
Template Border 9 C: Cut 16 in GP17BL.
Corner Posts: Cut 4 squares 7⁵/₈in x 7⁵/₈in (19.25cm x 19.25cm) in LC03FB.

Piece a total of 36 9-patch blocks as shown in Diagram 7. Piece into 4 borders of 9 blocks using the template B and C patches to fill in the edges as for border 5. Add 1 border to each side of the quilt.

Join a corner post to each end of the remaining 2 borders and add to the quilt, as shown in Diagram 12.

Border 10: Plain
Cut 8 strips 3in (7.5cm) x the width of the fabric, join as necessary. Cut 2 strips 3in x 84¹/₂in (7.5cm x 214.5cm) and 2 strips 3in x 79¹/₂in (7.5cm x 202cm) in GP34BL.

Join 1 shorter border to each side of the quilt, then join 1 longer border to the top and bottom of the quilt.

Binding: Cut 9³/₄yds (8.9m) of 2¹/₂in (6.5cm) wide bias binding in GP32BL.

Backing: Cut 2 pieces 45in x 90in (115cm x 229cm) in backing fabric.

FINISHING THE QUILT
Press the quilt top. Seam the backing pieces using a ¹/₄in (6mm) seam allowance to form a piece approx. 90in x 90in (229cm x 229cm). Layer the quilt top, batting and backing and baste together (see page 120). Using a toning machine quilting thread, quilt in the ditch around all the patch shapes and add embellishments if you wish. Trim the quilt edges and attach the binding (see page 121).

Diagram 9

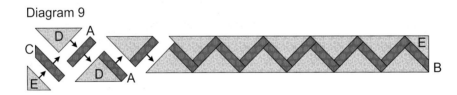

Diagram 10

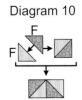

Diagram 11

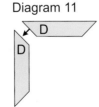

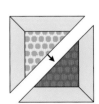

Diagram 12

Border 10

Border 9

Border 8

A
C
B

B A

9   5   1

2   6   10

4

8

12

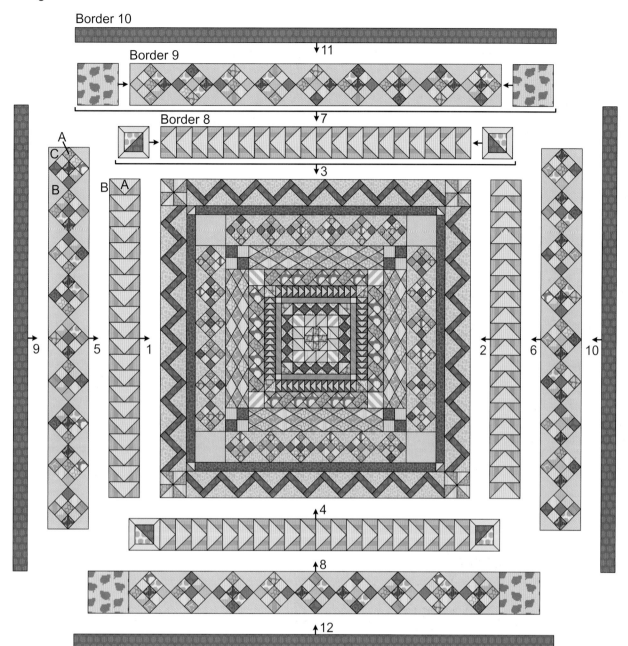
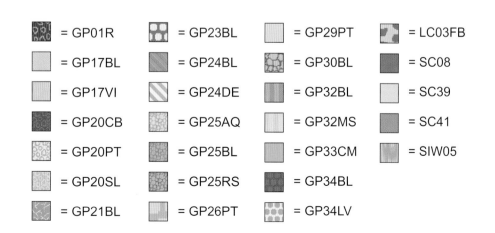

	= GP01R		= GP23BL		= GP29PT		= LC03FB
	= GP17BL		= GP24BL		= GP30BL		= SC08
	= GP17VI		= GP24DE		= GP32BL		= SC39
	= GP20CB		= GP25AQ		= GP32MS		= SC41
	= GP20PT		= GP25BL		= GP33CM		= SIW05
	= GP20SL		= GP25RS		= GP34BL		
	= GP21BL		= GP26PT		= GP34LV		

Templates

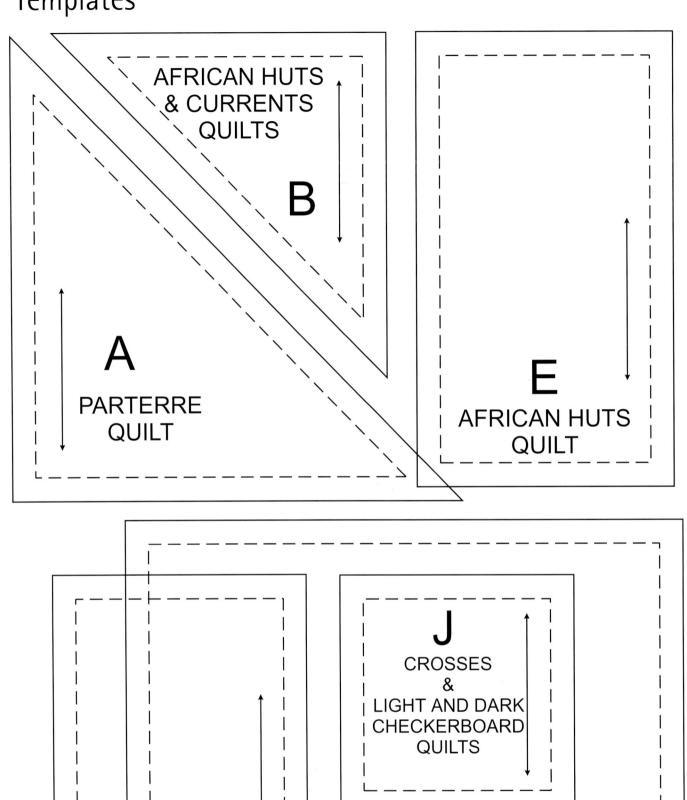

B
AFRICAN HUTS
& CURRENTS
QUILTS

A
PARTERRE
QUILT

E
AFRICAN HUTS
QUILT

F
AFRICAN HUTS
QUILT

J
CROSSES
&
LIGHT AND DARK
CHECKERBOARD
QUILTS

D
AFRICAN HUTS
QUILT

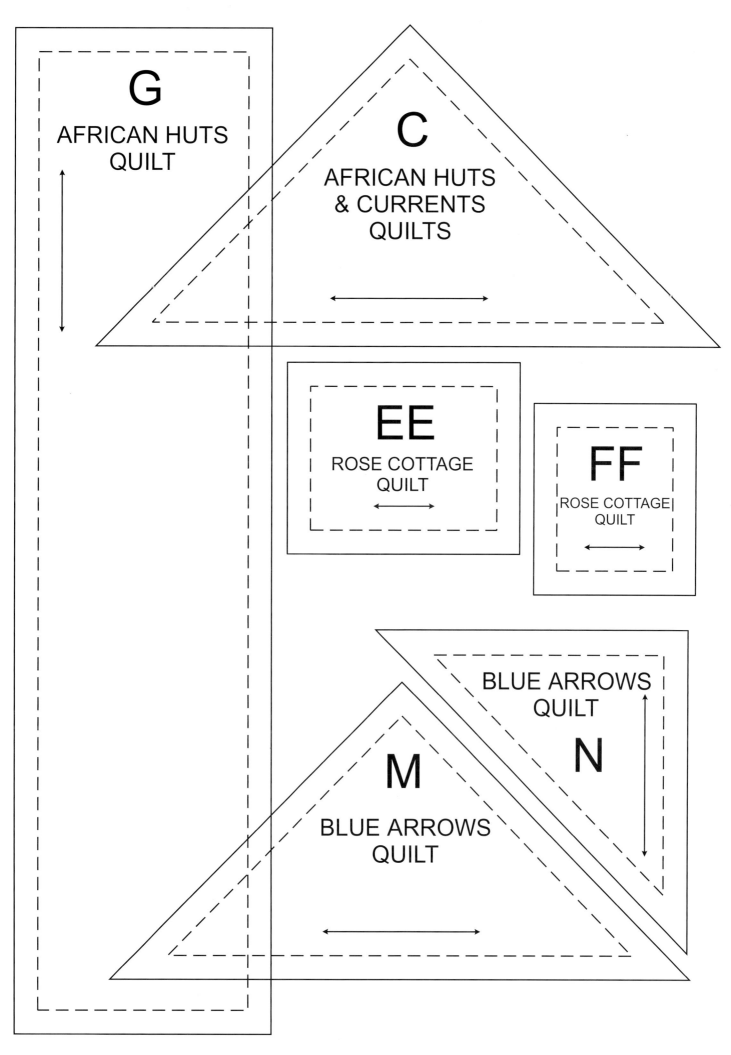

G
AFRICAN HUTS
QUILT

C
AFRICAN HUTS
& CURRENTS
QUILTS

EE
ROSE COTTAGE
QUILT

FF
ROSE COTTAGE
QUILT

BLUE ARROWS
QUILT
N

M
BLUE ARROWS
QUILT

I

FLORAL CHECKERBOARD QUILT

H

FLORAL CHECKERBOARD QUILT

Templates for Floral Checkerboard Quilt are printed at 50% of real size.
To use, scale them up 200% on a photocopier

104

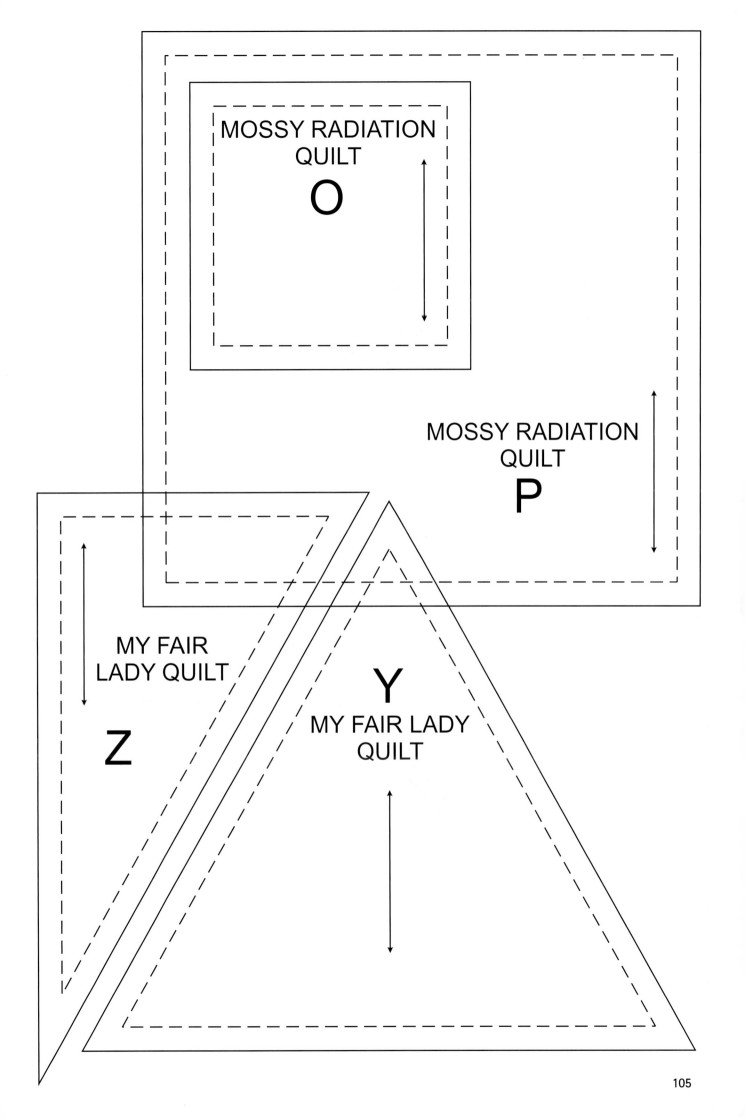

MOSSY RADIATION
QUILT

O

MOSSY RADIATION
QUILT

P

MY FAIR
LADY QUILT

Z

Y

MY FAIR LADY
QUILT

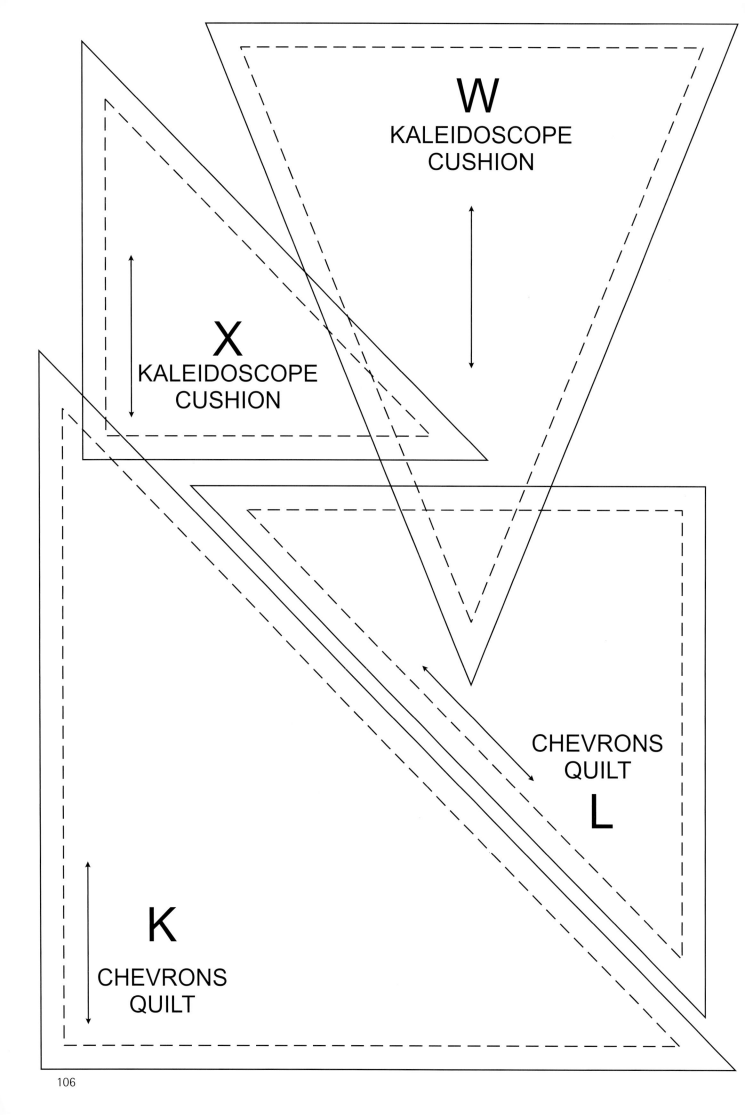

W
KALEIDOSCOPE
CUSHION

X
KALEIDOSCOPE
CUSHION

CHEVRONS
QUILT

L

K
CHEVRONS
QUILT

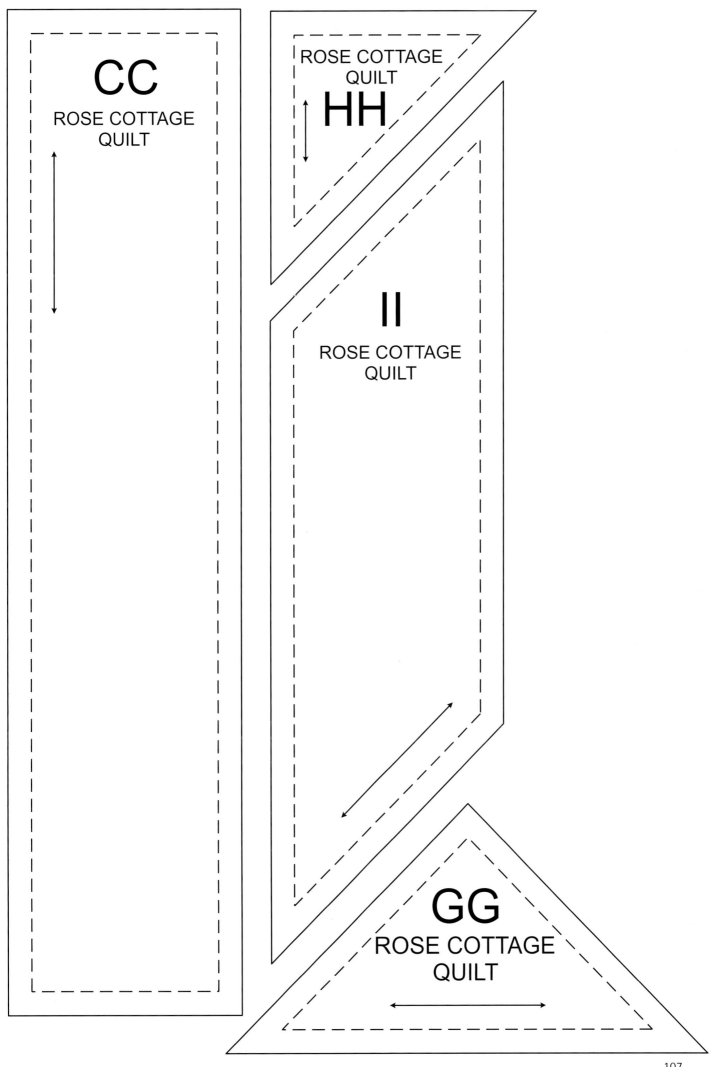

CC
ROSE COTTAGE
QUILT

ROSE COTTAGE
QUILT
HH

II
ROSE COTTAGE
QUILT

GG
ROSE COTTAGE
QUILT

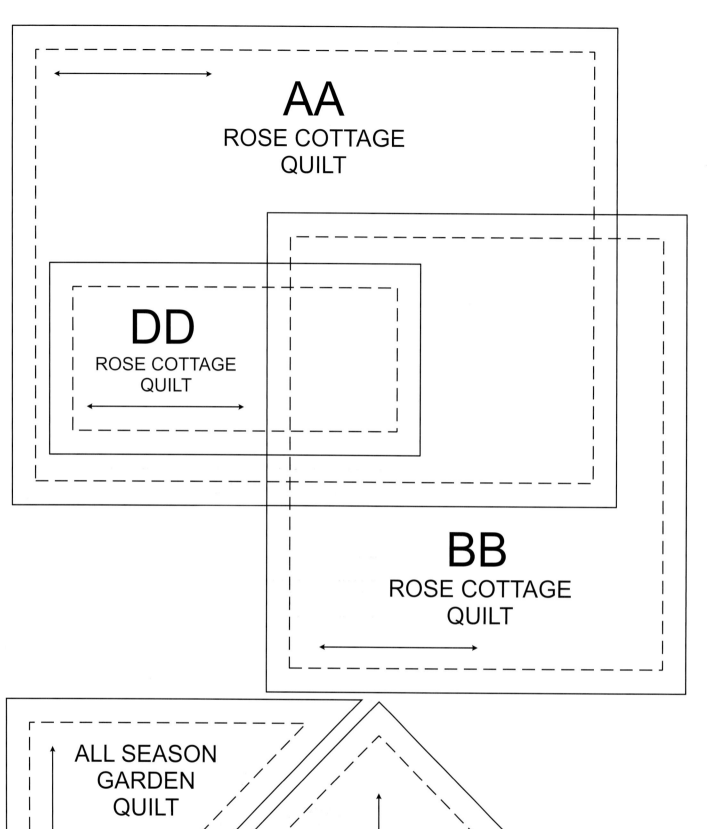

AA
ROSE COTTAGE
QUILT

DD
ROSE COTTAGE
QUILT

BB
ROSE COTTAGE
QUILT

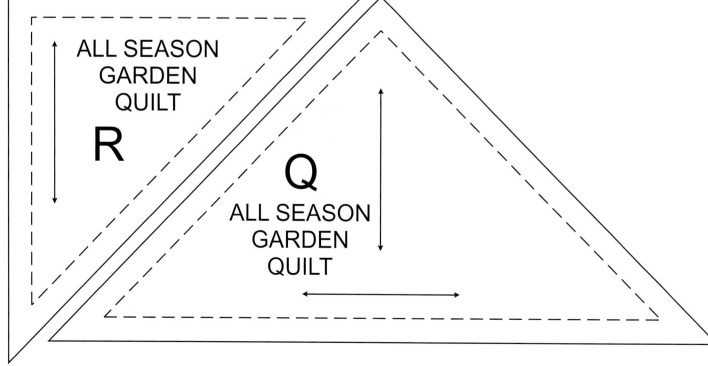

ALL SEASON
GARDEN
QUILT

R

Q
ALL SEASON
GARDEN
QUILT

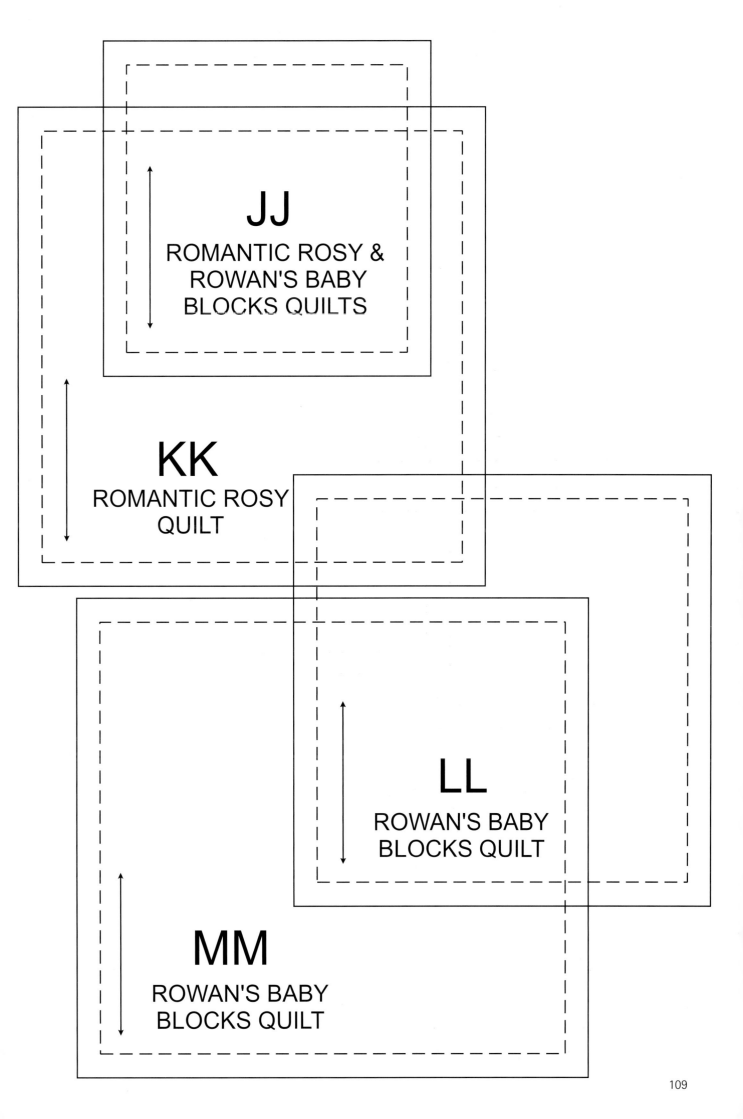

JJ

ROMANTIC ROSY &
ROWAN'S BABY
BLOCKS QUILTS

KK

ROMANTIC ROSY
QUILT

LL

ROWAN'S BABY
BLOCKS QUILT

MM

ROWAN'S BABY
BLOCKS QUILT

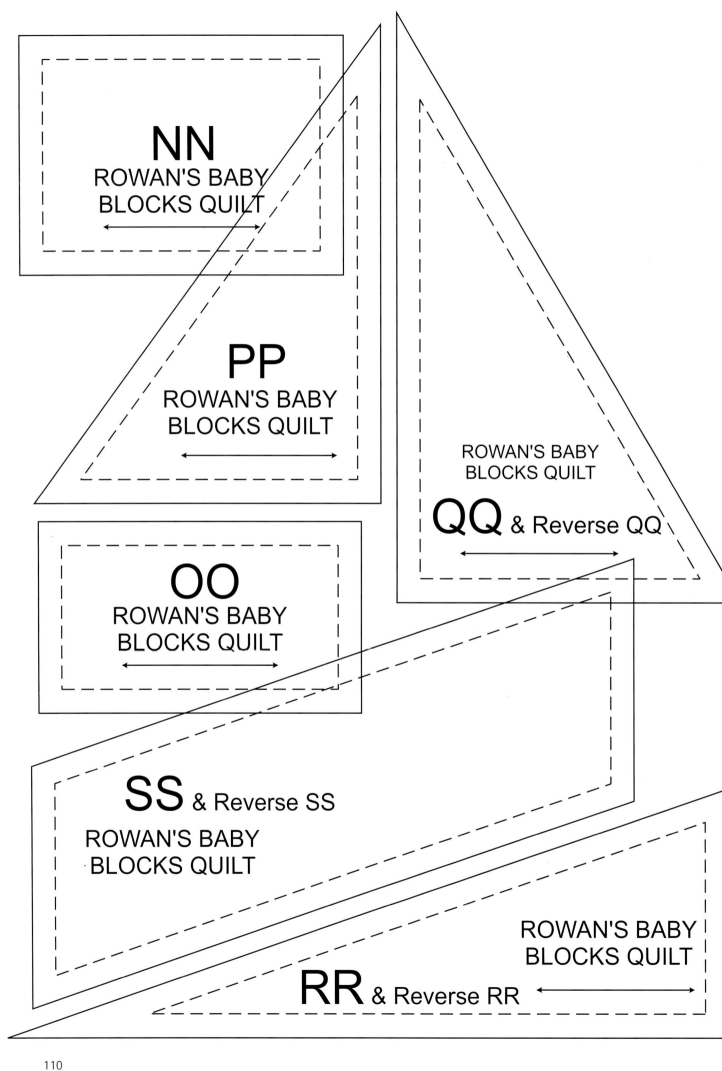

NN
ROWAN'S BABY
BLOCKS QUILT

PP
ROWAN'S BABY
BLOCKS QUILT

ROWAN'S BABY
BLOCKS QUILT
QQ & Reverse QQ

OO
ROWAN'S BABY
BLOCKS QUILT

SS & Reverse SS
ROWAN'S BABY
BLOCKS QUILT

ROWAN'S BABY
BLOCKS QUILT
RR & Reverse RR

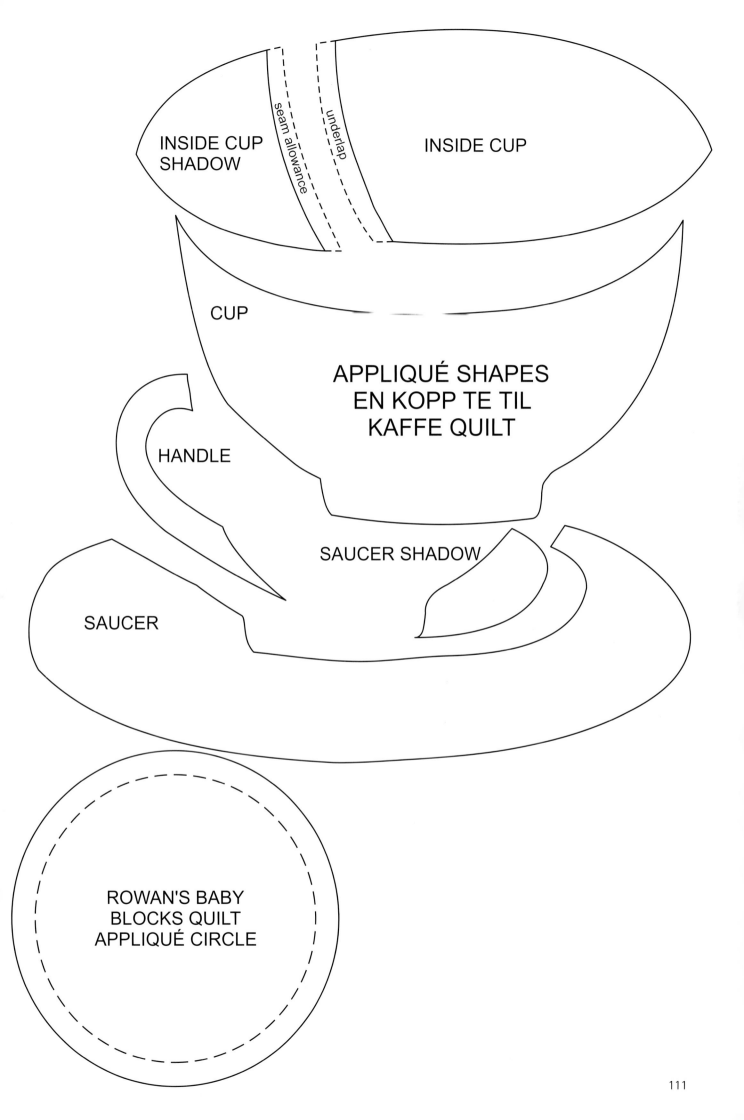

INSIDE CUP SHADOW

seam allowance

underlap

INSIDE CUP

CUP

APPLIQUÉ SHAPES
EN KOPP TE TIL
KAFFE QUILT

HANDLE

SAUCER SHADOW

SAUCER

ROWAN'S BABY
BLOCKS QUILT
APPLIQUÉ CIRCLE

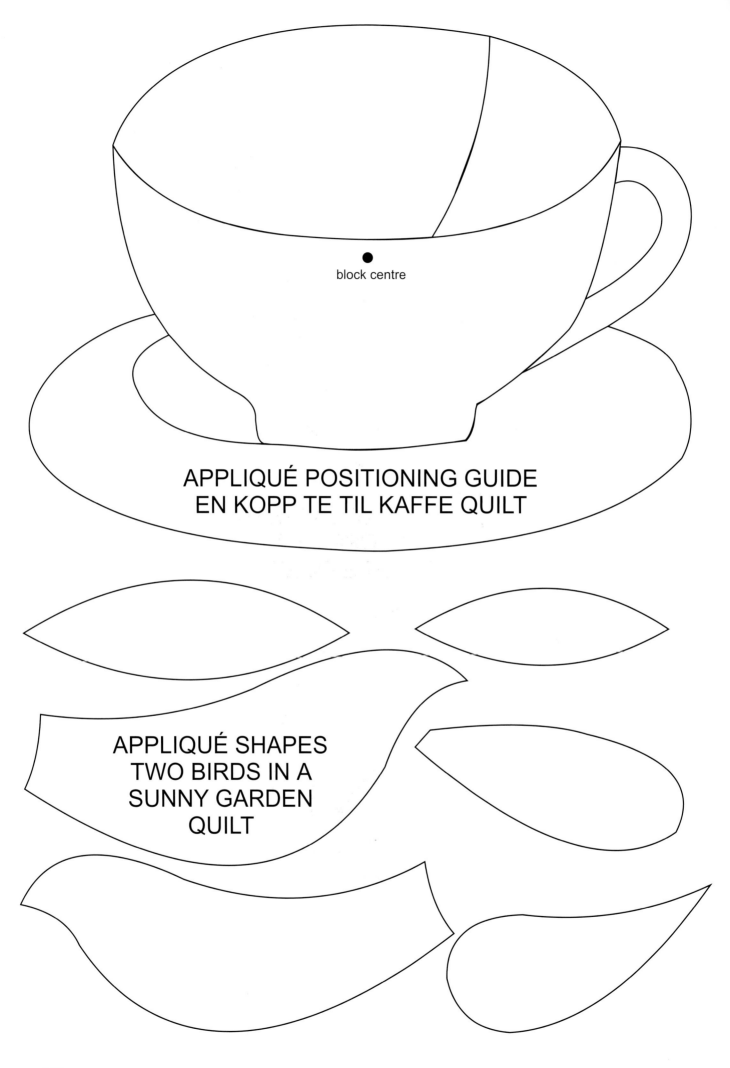

block centre

APPLIQUÉ POSITIONING GUIDE
EN KOPP TE TIL KAFFE QUILT

APPLIQUÉ SHAPES
TWO BIRDS IN A
SUNNY GARDEN
QUILT

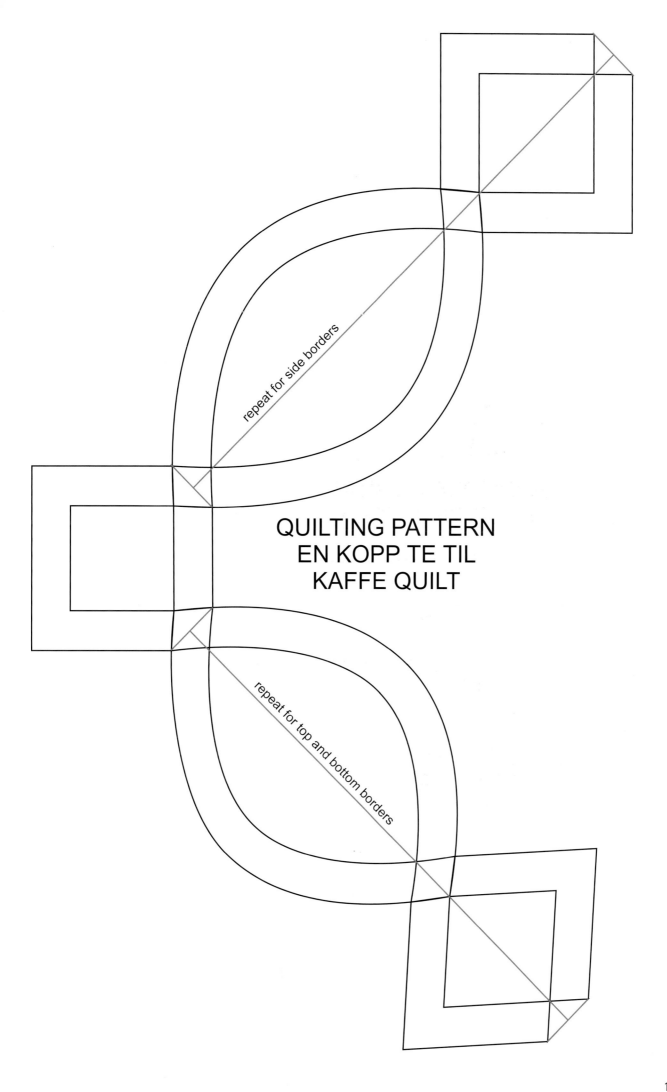

QUILTING PATTERN
EN KOPP TE TIL
KAFFE QUILT

repeat for side borders

repeat for top and bottom borders

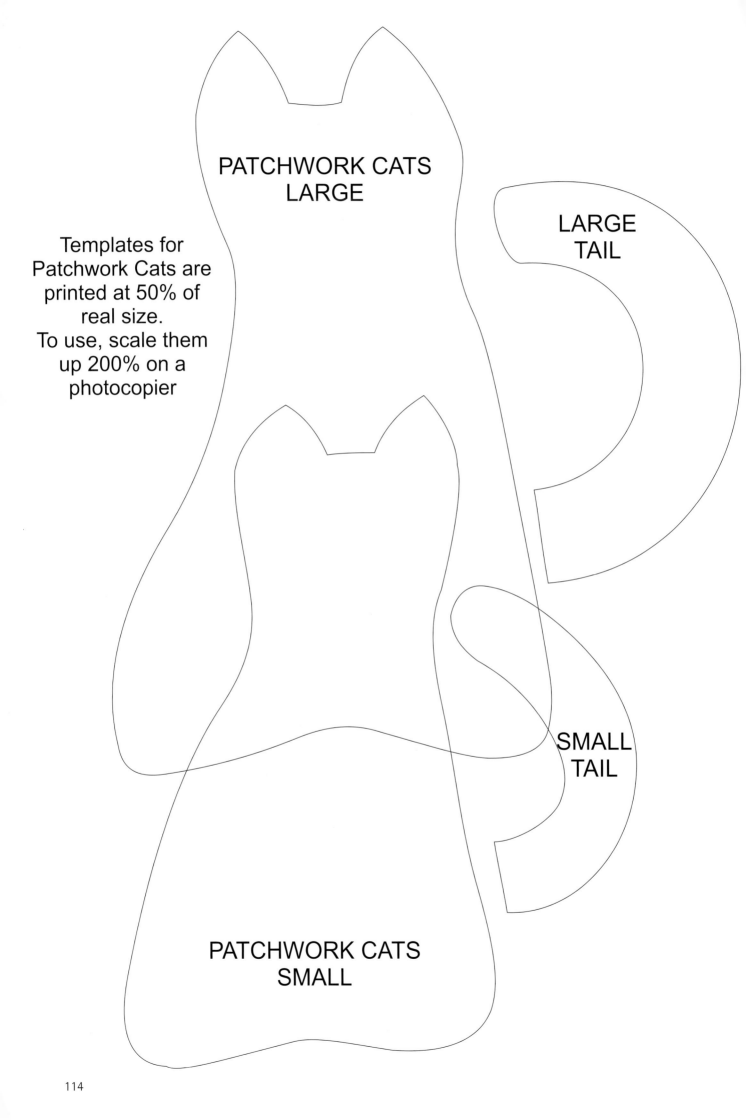

PATCHWORK CATS
LARGE

LARGE
TAIL

Templates for
Patchwork Cats are
printed at 50% of
real size.
To use, scale them
up 200% on a
photocopier

SMALL
TAIL

PATCHWORK CATS
SMALL

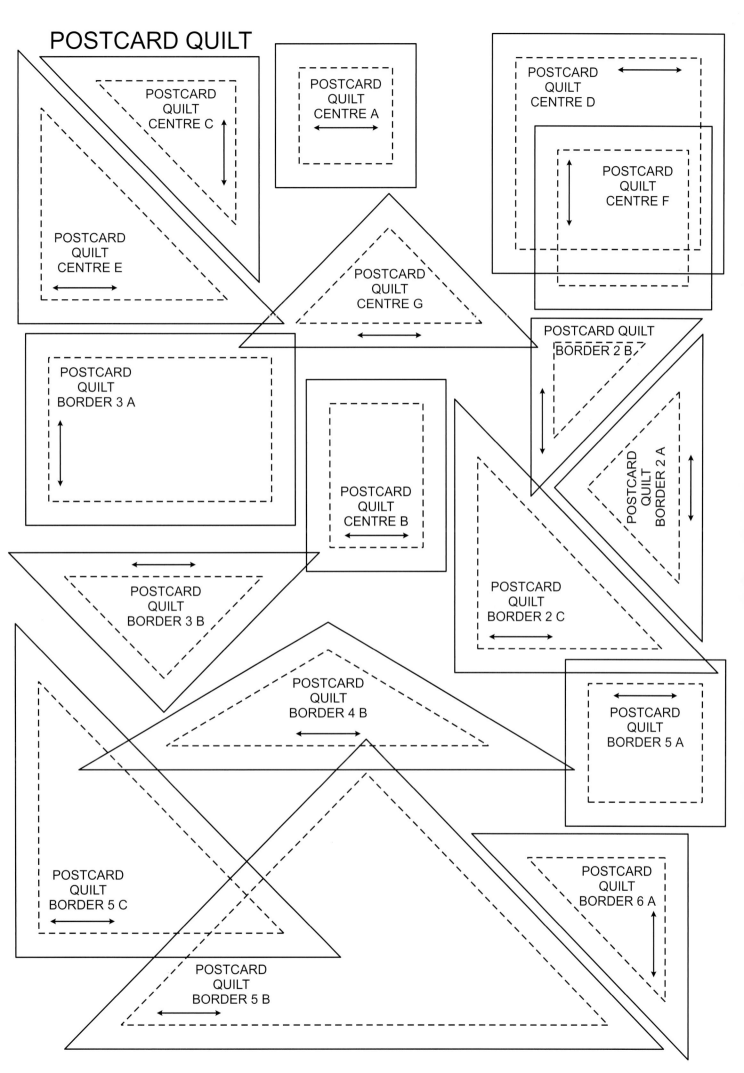

POSTCARD QUILT

POSTCARD QUILT

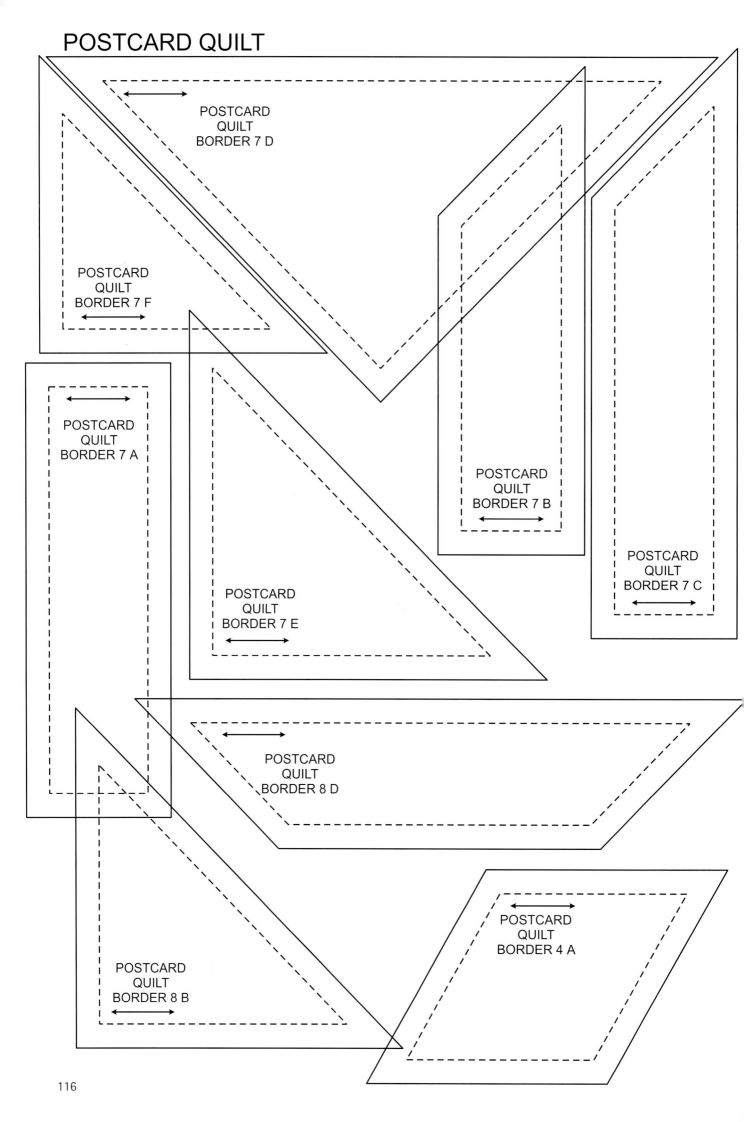

POSTCARD
QUILT
BORDER 7 D

POSTCARD
QUILT
BORDER 7 F

POSTCARD
QUILT
BORDER 7 A

POSTCARD
QUILT
BORDER 7 B

POSTCARD
QUILT
BORDER 7 C

POSTCARD
QUILT
BORDER 7 E

POSTCARD
QUILT
BORDER 8 D

POSTCARD
QUILT
BORDER 4 A

POSTCARD
QUILT
BORDER 8 B

POSTCARD QUILT

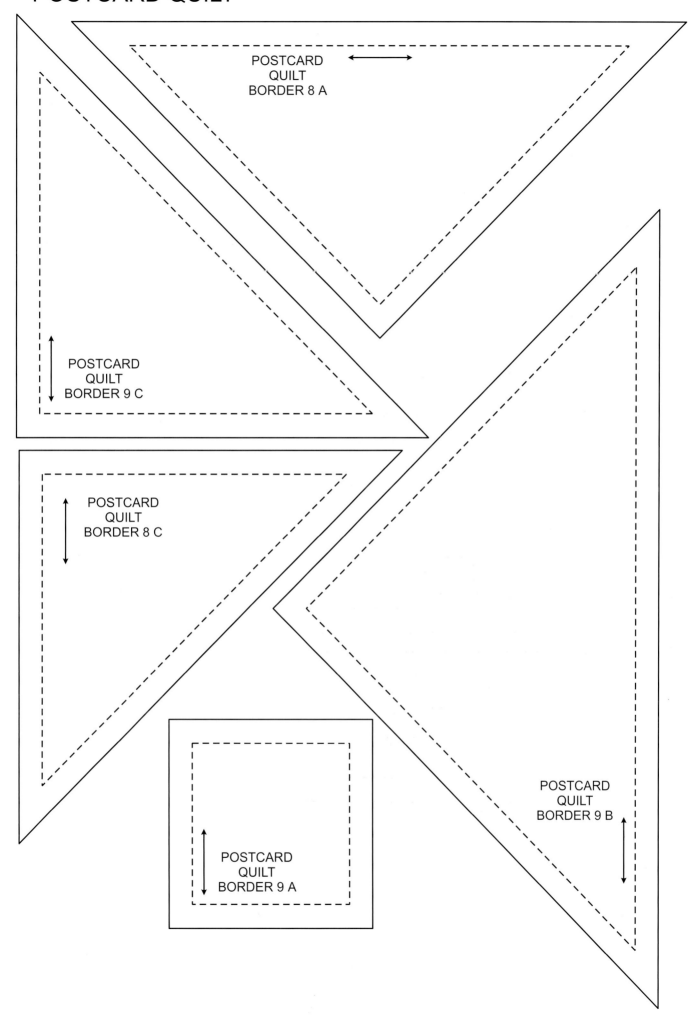

POSTCARD
QUILT
BORDER 8 A

POSTCARD
QUILT
BORDER 9 C

POSTCARD
QUILT
BORDER 8 C

POSTCARD
QUILT
BORDER 9 B

POSTCARD
QUILT
BORDER 9 A

Patchwork Know How

These instructions are intended for the novice quilt maker, providing the basic information needed to make the projects in this book, along with some useful tips.

Preparing the fabric

Prewash all new fabrics before you begin, to ensure that there will be no uneven shrinkage and no bleeding of colours when the quilt is laundered. Press the fabric whilst it is still damp to return crispness to it.

Making templates

Transparent template plastic is the best material, it is durable and allows you to see the fabric and select certain motifs. You can also use thin stiff cardboard.

Templates for machine piecing

1 Trace off the actual-sized template provided either directly on to template plastic, or tracing paper, and then on to thin cardboard. Use a ruler to help you trace off the straight cutting line, dotted seam line and grainlines. Some of the templates in this book are printed at 50% of real size, you will need to scale them up 200% on a photocopier.

2 Cut out the traced off template using a craft knife, ruler and a self-healing cutting mat.

3 Punch holes in the corners of the template, at each point on the seam line, using a hole punch.

Templates for hand piecing

• Make a template as for machine piecing, but do not trace off the cutting line. Use the dotted seam line as the outer edge of the template.

• This template allows you to draw the seam lines directly on to the fabric. The seam allowances can then be cut by eye around the patch.

Cutting the fabric

On the individual instructions for each patchwork, you will find a summary of all the patch shapes used.
Always mark and cut out any border and binding strips first, followed by the largest patch shapes and finally the smallest ones, to make the most efficient use of your fabric. The border and binding strips are best cut using a rotary cutter.

Rotary cutting

Rotary cut strips are usually cut across the fabric from selvedge to selvedge.

1 Before beginning to cut, press out any folds or creases in the fabric. If you are cutting a large piece of fabric, you will need to fold it several times to fit the cutting mat. When there is only a single fold, place the fold facing you. If the fabric is too wide to be folded only once, fold it concertina-style until it fits your mat. A small rotary cutter with a sharp blade will cut up to 6 layers of fabric; a large cutter up to 8 layers.

2 To ensure that your cut strips are straight and even, the folds must be placed exactly parallel to the straight edges of the fabric and along a line on the cutting mat.

3 Place a plastic ruler over the raw edge of the fabric, overlapping it about 1/2in (1.25cm). Make sure that the ruler is at right angles to both the straight edges and the fold to ensure that you cut along the straight grain. Press down on the ruler and wheel the cutter away from yourself along the edge of the ruler.

4 Open out the fabric to check the edge. Don't worry if it's not perfectly straight; a little wiggle will not show when the quilt is stitched together. Re-fold fabric, then place the ruler over the trimmed edge, aligning edge with the markings on the ruler that match the correct strip width. Cut strip along the edge of the ruler.

Using templates

The most efficient way to cut out templates is by first rotary cutting a strip of fabric the width stated for your template, and then marking off your templates along the strip, edge to edge at the required angle. This method leaves hardly any waste and gives a random effect to your patches.
A less efficient method is to fussy cut, where the templates are cut individually by placing them on particular motifs or stripes, to create special effects. Although this method is more wasteful it yields very interesting results.

1 Place the template face down on the wrong side of the fabric, with the grain line arrow following the straight grain of the fabric, if indicated. Be careful though - check with your individual instructions, as some instructions may ask you to cut patches on varying grains.

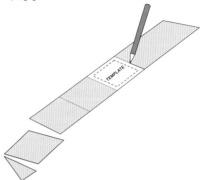

2 Hold the template firmly in place and draw around it with a sharp pencil or crayon, marking in the corner dots or seam lines. To save fabric, position patches close together or even touching. Don't worry if outlines positioned on the straight grain when drawn on striped fabrics do not always match the stripes when cut - this will add a degree of visual excitement to the patchwork!

3 Once you've drawn all the pieces needed, you are ready to cut the fabric, with either a rotary cutter and ruler, or a pair of sharp sewing scissors.

Basic hand and machine piecing

Patches can be joined together by hand or machine. Machine stitching is quicker, but hand assembly allows you to carry your patches around with you and work on them in every spare moment. The choice is yours. For techniques that are new to you, practise on scrap pieces of fabric until you feel confident.

Machine piecing

Follow the quilt instructions for the order in which to piece the individual patchwork blocks and then assemble the blocks together in rows.

1 Seam lines are not marked on the fabric, so stitch 1/4in (6mm) seams using the machine needle plate, a 1/4in- (6mm-) wide machine foot, or tape stuck to the machine as a guide. Pin two patches with right sides together, matching edges.

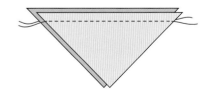

Set your machine at 10-12 stitches per inch (2.5cm) and stitch seams from edge to edge, removing pins as you feed the fabric through the machine.

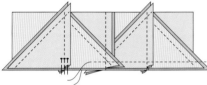

2 Press the seams of each patchwork block to one side before attempting to join it to another block.

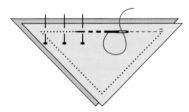

3 When joining rows of blocks, make sure that adjacent seam allowances are pressed in opposite directions to reduce bulk and make matching easier. Pin pieces together directly through the stitch line and to the right and left of the seam. Remove pins as you sew. Continue pressing seams to one side as you work.

Hand piecing

1 Pin two patches with right sides together, so that the marked seam lines are facing outwards.

2 Using a single strand of strong thread, secure the corner of a seam line with a couple of back stitches.

3 Sew running stitches along the marked line, working 8-10 stitches per inch (2.5cm) and ending at the opposite seam line corner with a few back stitches. When hand piecing never stitch over the seam allowances.

4 Press the seams to one side, as shown in machine piecing (Step 2).

Inset seams.

In some patchwork layouts a patch will have to be sewn into an angled corner formed by the joining of two other patches. Use the following method whether you are machine or hand piecing. Don't be intimidated - this is not hard to do once you have learned a couple of techniques. The seam is sewn from the centre outwards in two halves to ensure that no tucks appear at the centre.

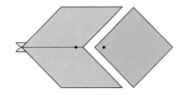

1 Mark with dots exactly where the inset will be joined and mark the seam lines on the wrong side of the fabric on the inset patch.

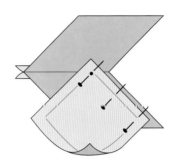

2 With right sides together and inset piece on top, pin through the dots to match the inset points. Pin the rest of the seam at right angles to the stitching line, along one edge of an adjoining patch.

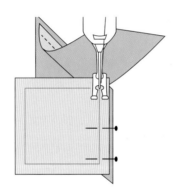

3 Stitch the patch in place along the seam line starting with the needle down through the inset point dots. Secure thread with a backstitch if hand piecing, or stitch forward for a few stitches before backstitching, when machine piecing.

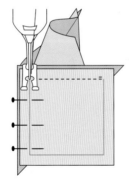

4 Pivot the patch, to enable it to align with the adjacent side of the angled corner, allowing you work on the second half of the seam. Starting with a pin at the inset point once again. Pin and stitch the second side in place, as before. Check seams and press carefully.

Hand appliqué

Good preparation is essential for speedy and accurate hand appliqué. The finger-pressing method is suitable for needle-turning application, used for simple shapes like leaves and flowers. Using a card template is the best method for bold simple motifs such as circles.

Finger-pressing:

1 To make your template, transfer the appliqué design on to stiff card using carbon paper, and cut out template. Trace around the outline of your appliquéd shape on to the right side of your fabric using a well sharpened pencil. Cut out shapes, adding a 1/4 in (6mm) seam allowance all around by eye.

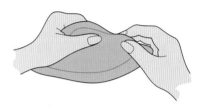

2 Hold shape right side up and fold under the seam, turning along your drawn line, pinch to form a crease. Dampening the fabric makes this very easy. When using shapes with 'points' such as leaves turn the seam allowance at the 'point' in first as shown in the diagram, then continue all round the shape. If your shapes have sharp curves you can snip the seam allowance to ease the curve. Take care not to stretch the appliqué shapes as you work.

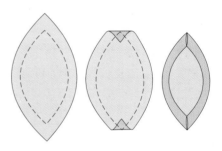

Card templates:

1 Cut out appliqué shapes as shown in step 1 of finger-pressing. Make a circular template from thin cardboard, without seam allowances.

2 Using a matching thread, work a row of running stitches close to the edge of the fabric circle. Place thin cardboard template in the centre of the fabric circle on the wrong side of the fabric.

3 Carefully pull up the running stitches to gather up the edge of the fabric circle around the cardboard template. Press, so that no puckers or tucks appear on the right side. Then, carefully pop out the cardboard template without distorting the fabric shape.

Pressing stems:
For straight stems, place fabric strip face down and simply press over the $^1/_4$ in (6mm) seam turning along each edge.

Needle-turning application

1 Take the appliqué shape and pin in position. Stroke the seam allowance under with the tip of the needle as far as the creased pencil line, and hold securely in place with your thumb. Using a matching thread, bring the needle up from the back of the block into the edge of the shape and proceed to blind-hem in place. This is a stitch where the motifs appear to be held on invisibly. Bring the thread out from below through the folded edge of the motif, never on the top. The stitches must be worked small, even and close together to prevent the seam allowance from unfolding and frayed edges appearing. Try to avoid pulling the stitches too tight, as this will cause the motifs to pucker up. Work around the whole shape, stroking under each small section before sewing.

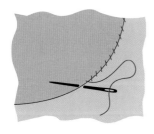

Quilting and finishing

When you have finished piecing your patchwork and added any borders, press it carefully. It is now ready for quilting.

Marking quilting designs and motifs

Many tools are available for marking quilting patterns, check the manufacturer's instructions for use and test on scraps of fabric from your project. Use an acrylic ruler for marking straight lines.

Stencils: Some designs require stencils, these can be made at home, by transferring the designs on to template plastic, or stiff cardboard. The design is then cut away in the form of long dashes, to act as guides for both internal and external lines. These stencils are a quick method for producing an identical set of repeated designs.

Preparing the backing and batting

• Remove the selvedges and piece together the backing fabric to form a backing at least 3in (7.5cm) larger all round than the patchwork top.

• For quilting choose a fairly thin batting, preferably pure cotton, to give your quilt a flat appearance. If your batting has been rolled up, unroll it and let it rest before cutting it to the same size as the backing.

• For a large quilt it may be necessary to join 2 pieces of batting to fit. Lay the pieces of batting on a flat surface so that they overlap by approx 8in (20cm). Cut a curved line through both layers.

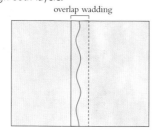

2. Carefully peel away the two narrow pieces and discard. Butt the curved cut edges back together. Stitch the two pieces together using a large herringbone stitch.

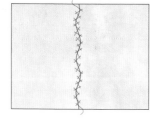

Basting the layers together

1 On a bare floor or large work surface, lay out the backing with wrong side uppermost. Use weights along the edges to keep it taut.

2 Lay the batting on the backing and smooth it out gently. Next lay the patchwork top, right side up, on top of the batting and smooth gently until there are no wrinkles. Pin at the corners and at the midpoints of each side, close to the edges.

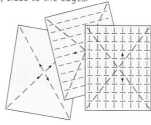

3 Beginning at the centre, baste diagonal lines outwards to the corners, making your stitches about 3in (7.5cm) long. Then, again starting at the centre, baste horizontal and vertical lines out to the edges. Continue basting until you have basted a grid of lines about 4in (10cm) apart over the entire quilt.

4 For speed, when machine quilting, some quilters prefer to baste their quilt sandwich layers together using rust-proof safety pins, spaced at 4in (10cm) intervals over the entire quilt.

Hand quilting

This is best done with the quilt mounted on a quilting frame or hoop, but as long as you have basted the quilt well, a frame is not essential. With the quilt top facing upwards, begin at the centre of the quilt and make even running stitches following the design. It is more important to make even stitches on both sides of the quilt than to make small ones. Start and finish your stitching with back stitches and bury the ends of your threads in the batting.

Machine quilting

• For a flat looking quilt, always use a walking foot on your machine for straight lines, and a darning foot for free-motion quilting.

• It's best to start your quilting at the centre of the quilt and work out towards the borders, doing the straight quilting lines first (stitch-in-the-ditch) followed by the free-motion quilting.

• When free motion quilting stitch in a loose meandering style as shown in the diagrams. Do not stitch too closely as this will make the quilt feel stiff when finished. If you wish you can include floral themes or follow shapes on the printed fabrics for added interest.

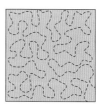

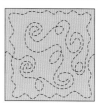

• Make it easier for yourself by handling the quilt properly. Roll up the excess quilt neatly to fit under your sewing machine arm, and use a table, or chair to help support the weight of the quilt that hangs down the other side.

Preparing to bind the edges

Once you have quilted or tied your quilt sandwich together, remove all the basting stitches. Then, baste around the outer edge of the quilt 1/4in (6mm) from the edge of the top patchwork layer. Trim the back and batting to the edge of the patchwork and straighten the edge of the patchwork if necessary.

Making the binding

1 Cut bias or straight grain strips the width required for your binding, making sure the grainline is running the correct way on your straight grain strips. Cut enough strips until you have the required length to go around the edge of your quilt.

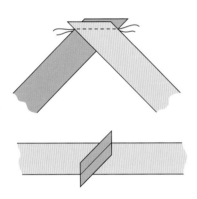

2 To join strips together, the two ends that are to be joined must be cut at a 45 degree angle, as above. Stitch right sides together, trim turnings and press seam open.

Binding the edges

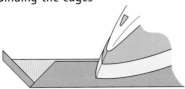

1 Cut starting end of binding strip at a 45-degree angle, fold a 1/4in (6mm) turning to wrong side along cut edge and press in place. With wrong sides together, fold strip in half lengthways, keeping raw edges level, and press.

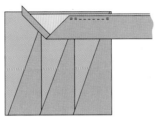

2 Starting at the centre of one of the long edges, place the doubled binding on to the right side of the quilt keeping raw edges level. Stitch the binding in place starting 1/4in (6mm) in from the diagonal folded edge (see above). Reverse stitch to secure, and working 1/4in (6mm) in from edge of the quilt towards first corner of quilt. Stop 1/4in (6mm) in from corner and work a few reverse stitches.

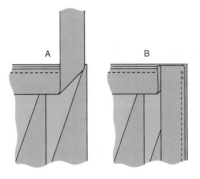

3 Fold the loose end of the binding up, making a 45-degree angle (see A). Keeping the diagonal fold in place, fold the binding back down, aligning the raw edges with the next side of the quilt. Starting at the point where the last stitch ended, stitch down the next side (see B).

4 Continue to stitch the binding in place around all the quilt edges in this way, tucking the finishing end

of the binding inside the diagonal starting section (see above).

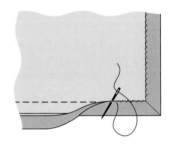

5 Turn the folded edge of the binding on to the back of the quilt. Hand stitch the folded edge in place just covering binding machine stitches, and folding a mitre at each corner.

Glossary of Terms

Appliqué The technique of stitching fabric shapes on to a background to create a design. It can be applied either by hand or machine with a decorative embroidery stitch, such as buttonhole, or satin stitch.

Backing The bottom layer of a *quilt sandwich*. It is made of fabric pieced to the size of the quilt top with the addition of about 3in (7.5cm) all around to allow for quilting take-up.

Basting or Tacking This is a means of holding two fabric layers or the layers of a *quilt sandwich* together temporarily with large hand stitches, or pins.

Batting or Wadding This is the middle layer, or *padding* in a quilt. It can be made of cotton, wool, silk or synthetic fibres.

Bias The diagonal *grain* of a fabric. This is the direction which has the most give or stretch, making it ideal for bindings, especially on curved edges.

Binding A narrow strip of fabric used to finish off the edges of quilts or projects; it can be cut on the straight *grain* of a fabric or on the *bias*.

Block A single design unit that when stitched together with other blocks create the quilt top. It is most often a square, hexagon, or rectangle, but it can be any shape. It can be pieced or plain.

Border A frame of fabric stitched to the outer edges of the quilt top. Borders can be narrow or wide, pieced or plain. As well as making the quilt larger, they unify the overall design and draw attention to the central area.

Butted corners A corner finished by stitching *border* strips together at right angles to each other.

Chalk pencils Available in various colours, they are used for marking lines, or spots on fabric.

Cutting mat Designed for use with a *rotary cutter*, it is made from a special 'self-healing' material that keeps your cutting blade sharp. Cutting mats come in various sizes and are usually marked with a grid to help you line up the edges of fabric and cut out larger pieces.

Free-motion quilting Curved wavy quilting lines stitched in a random manner. Stitching diagrams are often given for you to follow as a loose guide.

Fussy cutting This is when a template is placed on a particular motif, or stripe, to obtain interesting effects. This method is not as efficient as strip cutting, but yields very interesting results.

Grain The direction in which the threads run in a woven fabric. In a vertical direction it is called the lengthwise grain, which has very little stretch. The horizontal direction, or crosswise grain is slightly stretchy, but diagonally the fabric has a lot of stretch. This grain is called the *bias*. Wherever possible the grain of a fabric should run in the same direction on a quilt *block* and *borders*.

Inset seams or setting-in A patchwork technique whereby one patch (or block) is stitched into a 'V' shape formed by the joining of two other patches (or blocks).

Mitred Binding A corner finished by folding and stitching binding strips at a 45-degree angle.

Patch A small shaped piece of fabric used in the making of a *patchwork* pattern.

Patchwork The technique of stitching small pieces of fabric (*patches*) together to create a larger piece of fabric, usually forming a design.

Pieced quilt A quilt composed of *patches*.

Quilters' tape A narrow removable masking tape. If placed lightly on fabric, it provides a firm guideline for straight-line quilting patterns.

Quilting Traditionally done by hand with running stitches, but for speed modern quilts are often stitched by machine. The stitches are sewn through the top, *wadding* and *backing* to hold the three layers together. Quilting stitches are usually worked in some form of design, but they can be random.

Quilting hoop Consists of two wooden circular or oval rings with a screw adjuster on the outer ring. It stabilises the quilt layers, helping to create an even tension.

Quilt sandwich Three layers of fabric: a decorative top, *wadding* and *backing* held together with quilting stitches.

Rotary cutter A sharp circular blade attached to a handle for quick, accurate cutting. It is a device that can be used to cut up to six layers of fabric at one time. It must be used in conjunction with a 'self-healing' *cutting mat* and a thick plastic *ruler*.

Rotary ruler A thick, clear plastic ruler printed with lines that are exactly ?in (6mm) apart. Sometimes they also have diagonal lines printed on, indicating 45 and 60-degree angles. A rotary ruler is used as a guide when cutting out fabric pieces using a *rotary cutter*.

Sashing A piece or pieced sections of fabric interspaced between blocks.

Sashing Posts When blocks have sashing between them the corner squares are known as sashing posts.

Selvedges Also known as *selvages*, these are the firmly woven edges down each side of a fabric length. Selvedges should be trimmed off before cutting out your fabric, as they are more liable to shrink when the fabric is washed.

Stitch-in-the-ditch or Ditch quilting Also known as quilting-in-the-ditch. The quilting stitches are worked along the actual seam lines, to give a *pieced quilt* texture.

Template A pattern piece used as a guide for marking and cutting out fabric *patches*, or marking a *quilting*, or *appliqué* design. Usually made from plastic or strong card that can be reused many times.

Threads One hundred percent cotton or cotton-covered polyester is best for hand and machine piecing. Choose a colour that matches your fabric. When sewing different colours and patterns together, choose a medium to light neutral colour, such as grey or ecru. Specialist quilting threads are available for hand and machine quilting.

Walking foot or Quilting foot This is a sewing machine foot with dual feed control. It is very helpful when quilting, as the fabric layers are fed evenly from the top and below, reducing the risk of slippage and puckering.

Experience Ratings

★ Easy, straightforward, suitable for a beginner.

★ ★ Suitable for the average pachworker and quilter.

★ ★ ★ For the more experienced patchworker and quilter.

★ ★ ★ ★ Expert Level.

Printed Fabrics

When ordering printed fabrics please note the following codes which precede the fabric number and two digit colour code.

GP is the code for the Kaffe Fassett collection

CM is the code for the Carla Miller collection

LC is the code for the Lille collection

MN is the code for the Martha Negley collection

The fabric collection can be viewed online at the following **www.westminsterfibers.com**

Other ROWAN Titles Available

Kaffe Fassett's Caravan of Quilts

Kaffe Fassett's Quilt Road

Kaffe Fassett's Kaleidoscope of Quilts

Kaffe Fassett's Quilts in the Sun

The Impatient Patchworker

All Drima and Sylko machine threads,Anchor embroidery threads, and Prym sewing aids, distributed in UK by Coats Crafts UK, P.O. Box 22, Lingfield House, Lingfield Point, McMullen Road, Darlington, Co. Durham, DL1 1YQ. Consumer helpline: 01325 394237.

Anchor embroidery thread and Coats sewing threads, distributed in the USA by Coats & Clark, 3430 Toringdon Way, Charlotte, North Carolina 28277.Tel: 704 329 5800. Fax: 704 329 5025.

Prym products distributed in the USA by Prym-Dritz Corp, 950 Brisack Road, Spartanburg, SC 29303. Tel: +1 864 576 5050, Fax: +1 864 587 3353, e-mail: pdmar@teleplex.net

R O W A N

Green Lane Mill, Holmfirth, West Yorkshire, England
Tel: +44 (0) 1484 681881   Fax: +44 (0) 1484 687920   Internet: www.knitrowan.com
Email: mail@knitrowan.com

Biographies

Liza Prior Lucy

Liza Prior Lucy first began making quilts in 1990. She was so enthralled by the craftspeople she met and by the generously stocked quilt fabric shops in the States that quiltmaking soon became a passion. Liza originally trained as a knitwear designer and produced features for needlework magazines. She also owned and operated her own needlepoint shop in Washington, D.C. Liza met Kaffe when she was working as a sales representative for Rowan Yarns in the New York City area - Kaffe had come to America to promote his books and was working as Rowan's leading designer. They worked closely together in the States and the UK to write and produce the quilts for the books Glorious Patchwork and Passionate Patchwork.

Betsy Mennesson

Betsy began quilting and working with fabric in the late 90's. She found that piecing the quilt became the foundation of the project and that the free motion quilting made the design come alive. The movement within Kaffe's fabrics really inspired her free motion quilting. She particularly likes using the solid shot cottons from Kaffe's collections as backing, not only do the quilting designs really pop but it is like quilting through butter. Betsy lives just a few miles outside of Sisters, Oregon, home of the Stitchin' Post and the Sisters Outdoor Quilt Show. She has worked for and been inspired by the owner Jean Wells and her daughter Valori and has contributed quilts to a number of their books.

Hilde Aanerud Krohg

Hilde Aanerud Krohg started quilting in 1995, and finds designing quilts and working with colours a refreshing change from her job as a software engineer.

She has been an active member of her local quilting club for several years, and gets loads of inspiration from fellow quilters. Hilde likes to focus her designs around selecting colours that play well together and draws inspiration from paintings and artwork when working on her designs. She loves quilts with an antique look - simple designs where loads of fabrics in different colours and patterns are used. She is constantly searching for fabric, and is often seen in local quilt shops with her two small children "helping" out!

Hilde holds evening workshops in various techniques of working with colours and inspirations.
She is 36 years old, married with 2 children and lives outside Oslo in Norway.

Roberta Horton

Roberta Horton of Berkeley, California has been a quiltmaker for over 30 years. She has taught and lectured worldwide. Her study and love of quilts has pushed her into developing many workshops and to the authoring of six books. Roberta was the recipient of the 2000 Silver Star Award presented by the International Quilt Assosiation. This was in recognition of her lifetime body of work and the long-term effect it has had on quilting.

Brandon Mably

A regular contributor to the Rowan Patchwork books Brandon Mably has built a reputation as a quilt designer of simple, elegant quilts in restful colours. Brandon trained at The Kaffe Fassett Studio. He designs for the Rowan and Vogue Knitting magazine knitwear collections, and is the author of 'Brilliant Knits'.

Mary Mashuta

California quiltmaker Mary Mashuta has been making quilts and wearables for over thirty years. She is a professionally trained teacher who has been teaching internationally since 1985. Her classes always stress easily understood colour and design. She knows that no quilter can own too much fabric, and she enjoys discovering new blocks to showcase personal collections.

Pauline Smith

Pauline Smith has been a quilt maker since a college visit to The American Museum in Bath in 1968. With a successful business designing, making and selling patchwork through exhibition and commissions she has been involved in the development of patchwork at Rowan since 1998. Pauline designs by playing with the fabrics until she is happy with how they work together. During this process ideas for the quilt design emerge. As the Rowan patchwork co-ordinator, she works closely with Kaffe Fassett and everyone involved in producing the 'Patchwork and Quilting' series.

Keiko Goke

"It has been more than thirty years since my first encounter with quilts. I had looked at quilts published in Japanese magazines, thinking they were so interesting, and then, on my own, I began to create my own style. At the time, I never dreamed that I would have such a long relationship with quilts. I have won many awards in contests overseas and domestically. Quilting has given me many encounters with wonderful people and experiences. I am very grateful to have encountered quilting. It is my hope to freely and joyfully continue my relationship with quilts as long as my heart takes me in that direction."

Janet Bolton

Janet Bolton creates textile pictures using the simplest of techniques. Working directly with the fabrics she re-arranges the shapes and colours until the imagery is complete. Her inspiration comes from observation, imagination and memory. Janet exhibits world wide - Japan, Holland and America. She has been a visiting lecturer in London at the Victoria and Albert Museum and the Royal College of Art.
To find out more about Janet read 'A personal Approach' on pages 46-49.

Distributors and Stockists

Overseas Distributors of Rowan Fabrics

ARGENTINA
Coats Crafts Brazil
Rua do Manifesto,
705 Ipiranga
Sao Paulo
SP 04209-000

AUSTRALIA
XLN Fabrics
2/21 Binney Road,
Kings Park
New South Wales 2148
Tel: 61 2 96213066
info@xln.com.zu

AUSTRIA
Rhinetex
Geurdeland 7
6673 DR Andelst
The Netherlands
Tel: 31 488 480030
Email: info@rhinetex.com

BELGIUM
Rhinetex
Geurdeland 7
6673 DR Andelst
The Netherlands
Tel: 31 488 480030
Email: info@rhinetex.com

BRAZIL
Coats Crafts Brazil
Rua do Manifesto,
705 Ipiranga
Sao Paulo
SP 04209-000

CANADA
Telio
625 Rue DesLauriers
Montreal, QC, Canada
Tel: 514 271 4607
info@telio.com

CHILE
Coats Crafts Brazil
Rua do Manifesto,
705 Ipiranga
Sao Paulo
SP 04209-000

COLUMBIA
Coats Crafts Brazil
Rua do Manifesto,
705 Ipiranga
Sao Paulo
SP 04209-000

DENMARK
Coats HP A/S
Nannasgade 28
2200 Copenhagen N

FRANCE
Rhinetex
Geurdeland 7
6673 DR Andelst
The Netherlands
Tel: 31 488 480030
Email: info@rhinetex.com

GERMANY
Rhinetex
Geurdeland 7
6673 DR Andelst
The Netherlands
Tel: 31 488 480030
Email: info@rhinetex.com

HOLLAND
Rhinetex
Geurdeland 7
6673 DR Andelst
The Netherlands
Tel: 31 488 480030
Email: info@rhinetex.com

ICELAND
Storkurinn
Laugavegi 59
101 Reykjavik
Tel: 354 551 8258

ITALY
Coats Italy
Via Vespucci 2
20124 Milano
MILANO
Tel: 02 636 15224

JAPAN
Kiyohara & Co Ltd
4-5-5 Minamikyuhoji-Machi
Chuo-Ku
OSAKA
541-8506
Tel: 81 6 6251 7179

LUXEMBOURG
Rhinetex
Geurdeland 7
6673 DR Andelst
The Netherlands
Tel: 31 488 480030
Email: info@rhinetex.com

NEW ZEALAND
Fabco Limited
280 School Road
Waimauku
AUCKLAND 1250
Tel: 64 9 411 9996
info@fabco.co.nz

NORWAY
Coats Knappehuset AS
Pb 100 Ulset
5873 Bergen
Tel: 00 47 555 393 00

POLAND
Coats Polska Sp.z.o.o
ul. Kaczencowa 16
91-214 Lodz
Tel: 48 42 254 03 0400

PORTUGAL
Companhia de Linhas Coats & Clark
Quinta de Cravel
4430-968 Villa Nova de Gaia
Tel: 0351 223770700

SINGAPORE
Quilts and Calicoes
163 Tanglin Road
03-13 Tanglin Mall
247933
Tel: 65 68874708

SOUTH KOREA
Coats Korea Co Ltd,
5F Kuckdong B/D,
935-40 Bangbae-Dong,
Seocho-Gu, Seoul.
Tel: 82 2 521 6262

SOUTH AFRICA
Arthur Bales PTY Ltd
62 4th Avenue
PO Box 44644
Linden 2104
Tel: 27 11 888 2401

SPAIN
Coats Fabra
Sant Adria, 20
E-08030 Barcelona
Tel: 00 34 93 290 84 00

SWITZERLAND
Rhinetex
Geurdeland 7
6673 DR Andelst
The Netherlands
Tel: 31 488 480030
Email: info@rhinetex.com

SWEDEN
Coats Expotex AB
Stationsv gen 2
516 31 Dalsj fors
Tel: 46 337 207 900

TAIWAN
Long Teh Trading Co
No. 71 Hebei W. St
Beitun District
Taichung City
Tel: 886 4 2247 7711

UK
Rowan
Green Lane Mill
Holmfirth
HD9 2DX
United Kingdom
Tel: +44(0) 1484 681881
Internet: www.knitrowan.com
Email: mail@knitrowan.com

U.S.A
Westminster Fibers
3430 Toringdon Way
Suite 301,
Charlotte,
NC 28277
Tel: 704-329-5822
Email: fabric@westminsterfibers.com
Internet: westminsterfibers.com

currents quilt by Kaffe Fassett